SMALL BLOCKS,
STUNNING QUILTS

SMALL BLOCKS,

Martingale®
& COMPANY

STUNNING QUILTS

Mary Elizabeth Kinch and Biz Storms

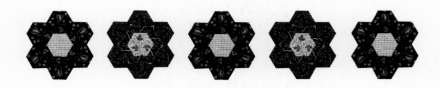

Small Blocks, Stunning Quilts

© 2008 by Mary Elizabeth Kinch and Biz Storms

That Patchwork Place® is an imprint
of Martingale & Company®.

Martingale & Company
20205 144th Ave. NE
Woodinville, WA 98072-8478 USA
www.martingale-pub.com

Printed in China
13 12 11 10 09 08   8 7 6 5 4 3 2 1

Library of Congress Cataloging-in-Publication Data
is available upon request.

ISBN: 978-1-56477-829-1

MISSION STATEMENT

*Dedicated to providing quality products
and service to inspire creativity.*

CREDITS

President & CEO: Tom Wierzbicki
Publisher: Jane Hamada
Editorial Director: Mary V. Green
Managing Editor: Tina Cook
Technical Editor: Darra Williamson
Copy Editor: Marcy Heffernan
Design Director: Stan Green
Production Manager: Regina Girard
Illustrator: Robin Strobel
Cover & Text Designer: Regina Girard
Photographer: Brent Kane

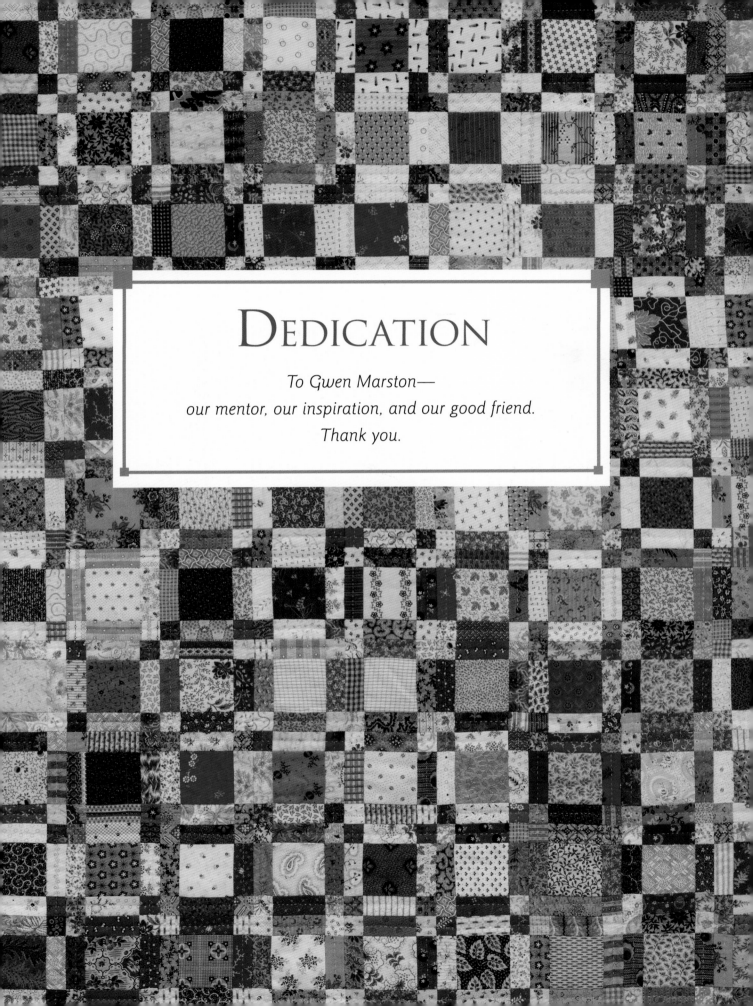

DEDICATION

To Gwen Marston—
our mentor, our inspiration, and our good friend.
Thank you.

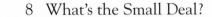

Contents

WHAT'S THE SMALL DEAL?

Making full-sized quilts from lots and lots and lots of small blocks has been a wonderful journey for both of us. The addictive nature of these small blocks—watching each one unfold into a captivating combination of color and fabric, and seeing the possibilities realized as the quilts grew—propelled us to explore, to challenge ourselves, and to test our hankering for small blocks. Here are our stories.

Detail of "Dining Room Stars," circa 1880. These quirky Star blocks—none larger than 4¾"—are wonderful examples of what "small blocks, stunning quilts" are all about. For a full view, see page 18.

Mary Elizabeth

Whenever I come across a bed-sized quilt made from small blocks, I stop in my tracks, mesmerized by the beauty in the balance of scale and proportion and awed by the tenacity of the quiltmaker. Time and time again I am drawn to these beautiful quilts, engaging in a dialogue of inquiry and learning and relishing the opportunity to study color combination, pattern, and design.

While quilts with blocks 6" or larger are common, small-block quilts usually have blocks that measure 4" to 5" or less; that is what makes them so rare and memorable.

Large quilts made with blocks of a relatively small size exist in all formats: strippy or row quilts, medallion-style, block-to-block, allover designs, samplers—even appliqué. I can easily close my eyes and picture breathtaking examples held in fine museums around the world, as well as orphan blocks—diminutive in size, but powerful in design—that I have noted in my design journal.

My first lessons about quilts came from the antique ones that adorned the beds at Black Creek Pioneer Village in Toronto, Ontario, where I worked as an historical interpreter during my teenage years. Dressed in period costume, sharing with visitors the details of pioneer life, I learned to piece together fabric for quilt tops and made my first very large, crude quilting stitches while sitting at a traditional quilt frame. My study and love of antique quilts has followed me since.

In about 1997, I discovered Gwen Marston's book *Liberated Quiltmaking* and instantly knew I had found a kindred quilting spirit. Over the years since, I have come to know Gwen, who has shared her passion and extensive knowledge of quilts, both antique and recent, with great generosity. She has ignited in me, through her example, a sense of creative fun and play. No longer afraid to experiment, I have definitely loosened up under her tutelage!

A diminutive (approximately 3½" x 3½") modified Framed Square block, which we discovered at vendor Jean Lyle's booth at the Chicago International Quilt Festival, sang to us in all its pinkness. Remade here in delicious Turkey red.

I met Biz Storms in 2002 through one of Gwen's Beaver Island Quilting Retreats where we became fast friends. We have enjoyed many trips together since and have spent hours quilting. We share a love of reproduction fabrics and beautiful vintage quilts. (It is so nice to email someone who will "get" the thrill of finding a new chrome yellow print or become equally breathless about an antique find.) We work wonderfully together, without ego, sharing ideas and concepts with great enthusiasm. I am blessed to know her.

It was at the first International Quilt Festival in Chicago that Biz and I hit what can be called nothing other than the mother lode of large, small-scale-block quilts. In a combination of exhibitions and vendors, we came across one outstanding example after another: an Ocean Waves crib quilt in blues, creams, and taupes; a Log Cabin quilt with logs a tiny ⅜" wide—it was heaven! Of course we came right home and, in the spirit of good pioneer quilters, set to making samples for our reference.

Detail of "Little Baskets," made by our mentor, Gwen Marston. Over the years Gwen has been generous in sharing her passionate and playful approach to quiltmaking, both qualities evidenced in the small-scale blocks in this colorful, full-sized quilt. For a full view, see page 25.

We soon learned that mere samples would not suffice; we would not be satisfied until we expanded our efforts into full-sized, small-block quilts. I can still remember the day when the 1"-wide bars on my Puss in the Corner blocks began to look a little "chunky," while the 5" finished block seemed positively gargantuan! I was hooked.

Of course, a return to Chicago was a must. I recall well the quickening of my pulse when I came upon "Four Play" (page 15). The quilt was captivating—a visual feast! It propelled us to continue to examine our love affair with small-block quilts. We were intrigued with the lessons they taught us.

Contrary to what you may think, small-block quilts can be far from busy or chaotic in nature. Although their origins may have been humble, born of the pioneer spirit of "use it up," these quilts exude life through the sheer multiplicity of blocks, the variety of fabrics, and the creation of pattern, texture, depth, and movement, as the eye wanders across the surface, taking it all in. Blocks small in relative scale to the finished quilt offer ample opportunity for an exploration of color. This exploration can manifest in fearless and loud combinations that dance before the eye, or as delicate and intricate plays of color that blend serenely for a calming effect.

While I tend to approach my quiltmaking in a very instinctual manner, I also have a naturally strong curiosity about why and how things work. I wondered what about this genre of quilt so appealed to the human heart and eye. What I noticed first is a soothing quality created by the repetition of the block or the theme in these quilts. This repetition draws upon the design concept of unity, a quality that marks a work as being consistent and complete, and is essentially what makes our efforts of creation successful.

The full-sized, small-block quilts that attracted my attention used repetition to achieve unity, provide predictability, and create a sense of familiarity, offering ample opportunity to integrate and assimilate the information they present. Could it be this repeated opportunity for understanding, through the flow and rhythm of information, that attracted me—and so many others—to these quilts?

A second question followed naturally: What inspired those pioneer quilters to incorporate these principles instinctively to create such evocative patterns and works of artistic expression? For my answer, I needed to look no further than to the abundance of stars that dot the darkness of the night sky, the leaves on the tree in front of my house, the multitude of petals on the large balls of a hydrangea flower, or the blanket of blue scillia that covers my lawn in spring. Pioneer quilters instinctively drew inspiration from nature. They learned from nature's best ideas as they observed the world around them and created original expressive quilts.

So look around you for inspiration. Study old quilts, train your eye to new proportions, and imagine what has not yet been seen. Then, armed with your new knowledge, pick up some fabric, engage in a bit of creative play, and discover the possibilities that await when small-scale blocks and large-scale works combine to create stunning quilts. Hopefully this book will help you get started!

Detail of "Four Play," a quilt we spied in the booth of quilt dealer Cindy Rennels at the Chicago International Quilt Festival. Mary Elizabeth was thrilled that this quilt became part of Biz's collection—and that she has visiting rights! For a full view, see page 15.

Biz

Sometimes you see a quilt that just knocks you sideways. Your fingers instinctively reach for fabrics and you find yourself compulsively sewing your own version of what you've seen.

This was my experience when Mary Elizabeth and I attended the 2005 Chicago International Quilt Festival, and I came face-to-face with an antique Four Patch quilt (page 15) made with breathtakingly small blocks. It is no understatement to say I was mesmerized by the ½" squares and basically rendered speechless. Luckily, my husband's Visa card accompanied me to Chicago, and the antique quilt quickly became a precious part of my quilt collection. But it didn't stop there.

Over the course of that trip, I purchased homespun and reproduction prints in unusual colors to go with the fabrics already in my studio, and within days of returning home, I had rotary cut *thousands* of 1" squares. For several days, I simply stitched Four Patch and Nine Patch blocks. I wasn't just happy—I was delirious! These little blocks, with their ½" finished squares, were the quintessential size. Batches of blocks almost stitched themselves together. I began to fill a large plastic storage box, and before long many hundreds of blocks were ready for me to toss around like a fabric salad. Forget strip piecing; sewing these little squares together quickly became addictive and therapeutic. Everyone who saw my rapidly accumulating blocks immediately plunged in with both hands and began to play. You couldn't *help* touching them.

Detail of "Kathy's Quilt," inspired by a friend's antique Nine Patch Postage Stamp quilt. This version contains over 1,400 Nine Patch blocks, each measuring 1½" square! For a full view (and instructions), see page 42.

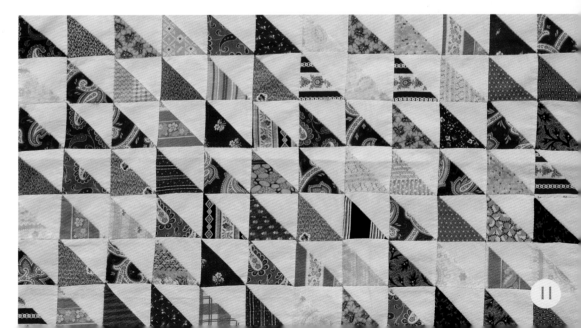

Detail of "Martha's Vineyard" quilt top, circa 1870. There is something soothing to the human eye in the repetition of a simple pattern. Alas, the maker of this quilt top—with its multitude of little half-square-triangle blocks—remains unknown. For a full view, see page 23.

Detail of the "Guest Room Quilt." The Broken Dishes block works well in both a 4" and 2" version, as demonstrated in Biz's quilt, a favorite when Mary Elizabeth comes to stay. For a full view (and instructions), see page 74.

As an unexpected yet rewarding side effect, I discovered that it was unbelievably calming to simply sit and stitch, square by square. I had forgotten the enjoyment of making something using more traditional methods, seeing the steady progress from my efforts. It was the kind of experience I don't have when I'm production sewing; that is, strip piecing with the pedal-to-the-metal. And, for a certified insomniac like me, quietly stitching on my Featherweight was a perfect way to be productive in those early hours before dawn.

Looking back over the quilts I have made in the last 10 years, it is clear that the size of the blocks has become steadily smaller—not to the miniature levels, but still in the neighborhood where some family members might question my sanity. Simple 6" blocks look better to me when they're scaled down to 3". More detailed blocks, previously stitched at 8", look quite podgy and tell me they need to be reduced to 5".

Postage Stamp quilts, which I had previously considered a charismatic yet questionable novelty, are now on my project list.

I've discovered that when I'm making small-scale blocks, I can make considerably more, which means I can include an even greater selection of fabric in a quilt top. To someone who considers fabric as important as chocolate and apples (see "About the Authors" on page 95), what could be better?

As I've worked on recent quilts, with their intimately sized blocks and myriad color and fabric combinations, I've found them to be much more enticing than my earlier efforts. I see lots of little details as the blocks and tops come together, some yummy and others not, which make the quilts incredibly unique. Moreover, the blocks are lighter, easier to handle, quick to stitch, simple to press, and fast to "groom." All things considered, these small-block quilts are really fun to sew.

Yet the best part of this creative journey is sharing it with my wonderful traveling companion and friend, Mary Elizabeth. Together we are compelled to make our quilt blocks smaller, our fabric choices more unusual (although still influenced by the antique), and not to preplan our blocks and quilt tops. Mary Elizabeth and I have spent thousands of hours together sewing, driving to museums and quilt festivals, and poring over antique quilts, reminding ourselves to breathe when necessary! We have laughed and had great fun in the process, and I look forward to our adventures ahead.

During the winter months of 2005, I stitched up Four Patch and Nine Patch quilt tops, and then launched into a Courtyard Steps Log Cabin quilt that features reproductions of fabrics from 1860 to 1880. I chose oodles of brown fabrics, along with pinks and shirting fabrics, and greens, purples, blues, and blacks to achieve the feel of an antique quilt. I think it's safe to say that this is one of my favorite quilts of all those I will ever stitch . . . and I knew it after the first 50 blocks. Now, if only I'd made its 5" blocks a

little smaller, as I did in my "Homestead Quilt" (detail below)!

The Four Patch and Nine Patch study quilts, and the Courthouse Steps quilt, are only three of the dozen or so small-block quilts I have made in the last handful of years, yet they are profoundly meaningful to me. They consolidate what I'd recognized on an instinctive level; small blocks are the cornerstone for creating stunning quilts. Regardless of whether you sew your blocks together in a planned or random way, and however you assemble the quilt top, when it's time to sew it all together, the key ingredient is the small block.

I piece and quilt in an intuitive way, sewing and experimenting with what feels right to me. Beyond that, I leave it alone and don't question why it feels right. As Freud purportedly once said, "Sometimes a cigar is just a cigar."

So give one of these small-block quilts a try. They're lots of fun. You get to play with your fabric, and the finished quilts are truly stunning.

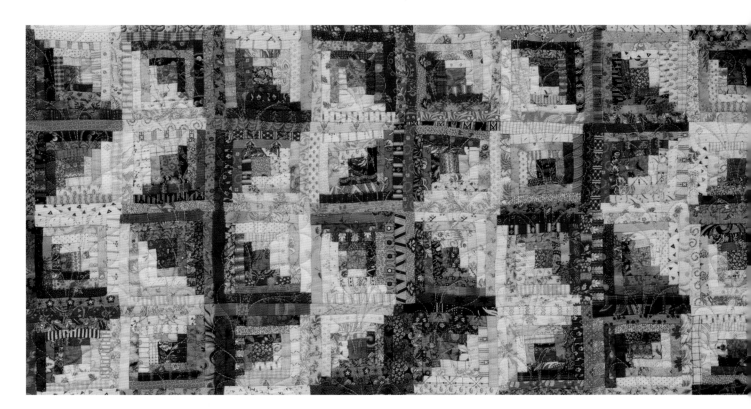

A detail of the "Homestead Quilt," which Biz made some time after the Courthouse Steps Log Cabin quilt described above. The finished "logs" in this quilt measure a mere ⅜" wide, and the finished block is just 3¾"! For a full view (and instructions), see page 62.

QUILTS THAT MAKE OUR HEARTS SING

When we think about small-block quilts, one of the first questions that arises is how these quilts came to be. Was the block size and pattern dictated by the limitations imposed by the small pieces of fabric available, or were the small pieces a deliberate design choice? The answer, not surprisingly, is both. A pivotal point between the choice of fabric at hand and a focus on design appears to be the late nineteenth century.

In the late 1700s and early 1800s, fabric was either produced in homes on hand looms or imported from England. By the 1820s, however, this had changed. Mills were appearing throughout the New England states, so that by the 1850s, large-scale domestic production was well underway.

Despite the improved availability of commercially produced fabric (and perhaps because of well-remembered scarcities in general and the continued scarcity and cost of fabric in rural areas), the majority of homes maintained a "piecing" or "scraps" bag, which received the remnants of fabric from making clothing and other household sewing. Sometimes from necessity, homemakers patched these bits together into quilts to keep their families warm. It was not uncommon for a frugal quilter to piece two small scraps of the same fabric together to obtain a piece large enough to complete the block.

A detail of the "Sugar Loaf Quilt," circa 1880. As you can see, lots and lots of little pieces went into the making of this quilt, owned now by Fumie Ono. For a full view, see page 21.

14

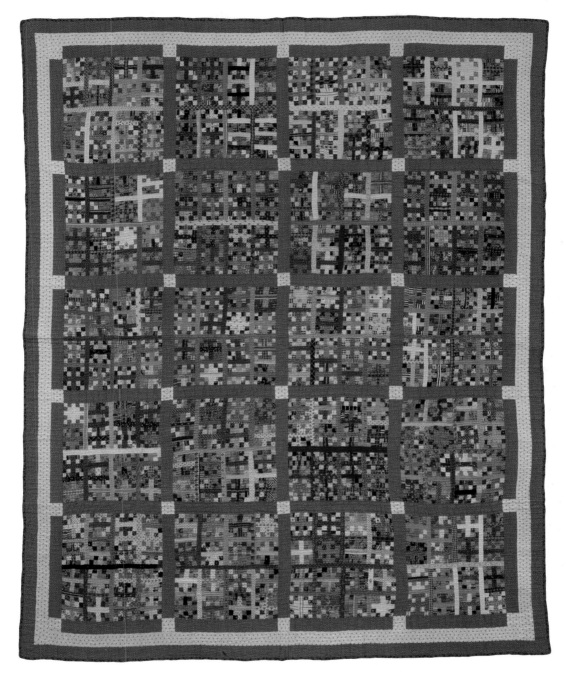

"Four Play," circa 1880, 64" x 81". Maker unknown. From the collection of Biz Storms. (Detail on page 10.)

Look at this: Tiny ½" blocks of muted colors are woven together with punchy red sashing. The quilt-maker began each large block with one small four-patch unit and multiplied the design exponentially. Biz notes that, could she meet the quiltmaker, she would like to ask if this was deliberate, or did it just happen?

What originally attracted Biz to the quilt—which she ultimately purchased—was the sheer volume of different fabrics and the many interpretations of the Four Patch block. We like the fact that blocks range from muted to vibrant and that the random piecing creates spontaneous secondary patterns. It appears the quiltmaker had a ball putting it all together and Biz never gets tired of looking at it. What is not visible in this photograph is the astonishing amount of quilting; freehand lines, spaced approximately ¼" apart, run horizontally across the entire quilt.

In her 1999 essays, "Blue Ridge Quiltmaking in the Late Twentieth Century" (see "Bibliography" on page 91), quilt historian Laurel Horton wrote about six interviews conducted with regional quiltmakers in 1978 as part of the Blue Ridge Parkway Folklife Project Collection, by the Library of Congress's American Folklife Center in cooperation with the National Park Service.

The women in these interviews learned their craft at the hands of their mothers in the early 1900s, continuing a long tradition of quilting wisdom being passed from generation to generation. This information included the source and use of fabric for quilts and described traditions quite different from our modern practice of buying new fabric specifically for quiltmaking. Quilters describe saving scraps left over from making clothing, getting scraps from neighbors and friends, and occasionally buying "cutaway" remnants from clothing factories where they could specify bags of lights or darks. One quilter, Mamie Bryan, recounts how, with limited access to materials, she did the best with what she had. "Large remnants were left large and were squared off to make them easy to join with others. Smaller scraps were saved up and combined to make tops."

As a child, another quilter, Mrs. Shockley, recalled being given paper diamonds cut by her mother along with just the smallest scraps and strings (narrow strips) for string piecing. "Anything over an inch, we didn't get hold of." Her mother then combined the string-pieced diamonds to make eight-pointed stars. In all, Mrs. Shockley remembered buying special fabric for only *two* quilts. Stories like these give us some insight into the proclivity for using up even the smallest bits of cloth in a quilt.

Late in the nineteenth century trends began to shift as abundance, not only in fabric, but in leisure time, caused the number of small-block quilts to increase dramatically. One Patch Charm quilts (quilts typically made without repeating a fabric), Crazy quilts, and what researcher Sue Reich calls "multitudinous" works were spurred on by reports in the press of the accomplishments of some quilters. The race to beat the latest record-breaking feat of quiltmaking was on! In a 2007 magazine article, "Multitudinous Scrap Quilts," Sue notes how "some writers expressed amazement at the quilters' achievements, some derided the activity as a waste of time, and some encouraged the stitchers to one-up each other." In the mid-1800s, it was not unheard of to see quilts made with 1,000 to 10,000 pieces reported as news items in local papers. In her book, *Quilting News of Yesteryear: 1,000 Pieces and Counting* (see "Bibliography"), Sue includes a notice from an 1834 Gettysburg, Pennsylvania, newspaper that recognizes a young lady in Charleston, South Carolina, for her "uncommon stock of patience and perseverance" as exhibited by the completion of "two great achievements of the needle: a Hexagon Quilt, composed of 7,630 pieces, and a Star Quilt composed of 7,239."

By 1880, earlier trends were met with an expanding fervor, and gradually these astounding numbers were surpassed. As the numbers grew, the scale of the blocks and pieces relative to the finished size of the quilt continued to shrink until, in the 1920s and 1930s, the competitive challenges taken up by many quilters saw *small* scale turn to *miniature* scale, and the number of pieces in these fantastical works climax in a frenzy of piecing between 1930 and 1950. (In the 1930s, Albert Small made his first quilt with 36,000

Detail of "Rocky Mountain Thimbles." The 6,500-plus "thimbles" in Biz's quilt measure a mere 1¼" tall, enabling her to honor the tradition of using just the smallest bits of fabric in her quilt. For a full view (and instructions), see page 30.

hexagons and his second with 63,467 hexagons!) The fever of competition culminated in 1948, when Grace Snyder completed her "Petit-Point Flower Basket" quilt with its 85,789 pieces.

With the decline in quiltmaking after World War II and the trend toward store-bought clothes, the scrap bag was no longer a commonplace fixture in many homes. As a result, the renewed interest in quiltmaking surrounding the bicentennial in 1976 launched the trend of purchasing fabric for the sole purpose of making quilts. Without the riot of scraps readily available, small-block quilts ceased to be—for the most part—necessity driven and instead became primarily the conscious design choice of the quilt-maker.

For our part, we leave the miniature-block, full-sized quilt endeavors to others and are very content to stay with small-scale-block quilts. We love studying small-block antique quilts, and we never cease to be amazed that no matter their state of wear, they always have some lessons to bestow. They continue to reinforce our profound respect for their makers. Some of our favorite quilts that have triggered our passion and fascination appear in the following pages. Enjoy!

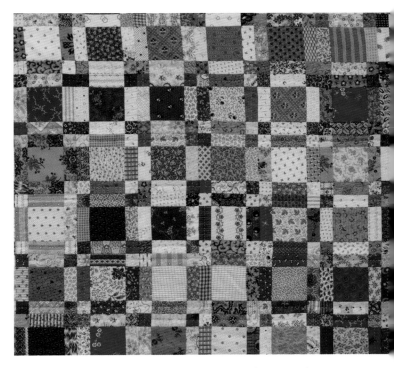

Detail of the "Farmhouse Quilt." Unlike many of their foremothers, Biz and Mary Elizabeth purchased most of the fabrics for the 3½" blocks in this full-sized scrap quilt, but you wouldn't know it from the incredible mix of prints found in the little pieces. For a full view (and instructions), see page 48.

LESSONS IN THE QUILTS

The biggest gift you can give yourself with regard to your quilting is the time to slow down and really *see* what is happening in the quilts you admire; that is, to look beyond your initial response to tap into exactly what attracts you. Here are some things to focus on to help develop the "seeing part" of your creativity and to guide you as you view the quilts throughout these pages:

- The size and shape of the quilt

- The scale and the proportion of the various elements: block size, sashing, setting, borders, and binding

- The balance of the design: Is it symmetrical or asymmetrical?

- The use of color

- The choice of fabric: Are there solids, prints, variety in scale and value? A great variety of fabrics or just a few?

- The presence of any secondary designs created by adjacent pieces or blocks, or by the use of the fabric (e.g., fussy cutting)

- The quilting style: Is it utilitarian, decorative, echoing, or canvas for artistic expression?

- The presence of spacer blocks, bars, or coping rows: Does their use change the pattern or the subsequent shape of the quilt?

- The batting used: Is it thick or thin?

- Surface techniques beyond quilting (e.g., trapunto)

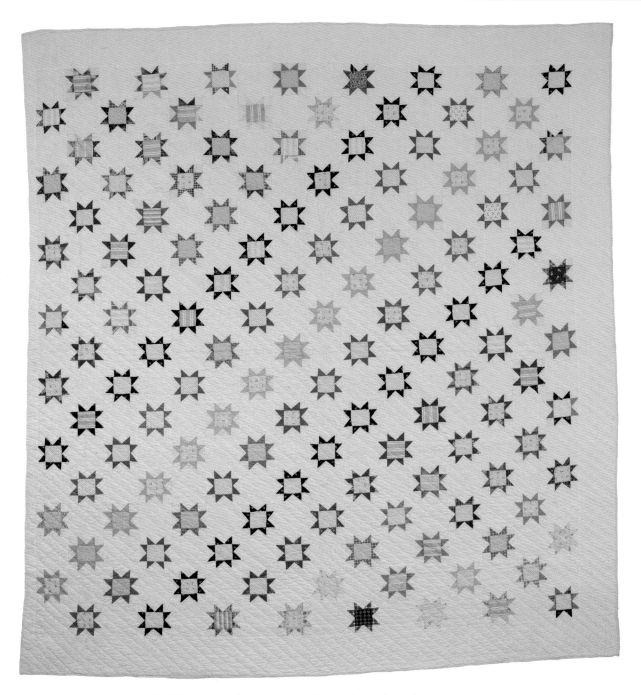

"Dining Room Stars," circa 1880, 77" x 88". Maker unknown.
From the collection of Biz Storms. (Detail on page 8.)

Look at this: Lots of anomalies here! The Star blocks range from 4¼" to 4¾" square, and—one of our favorite elements—the quilt has borders on just three sides. Another quirk: the maker started out ambitiously with double rows of quilting on one border, only to change abruptly to single diagonal lines across the remainder of the quilt. We suspect the quilting lines were done freehand as they are not precisely spaced and occasionally meander or split off into two lines of stitching. The quilter placed her colors astutely to form strong diagonal rows, lending sophistication to her design—an effect that lasted only as far as her supply of a specific fabric would stretch. Some star points have faded over time to blend with the background while others have remained bold, adding charm to this historical beauty.

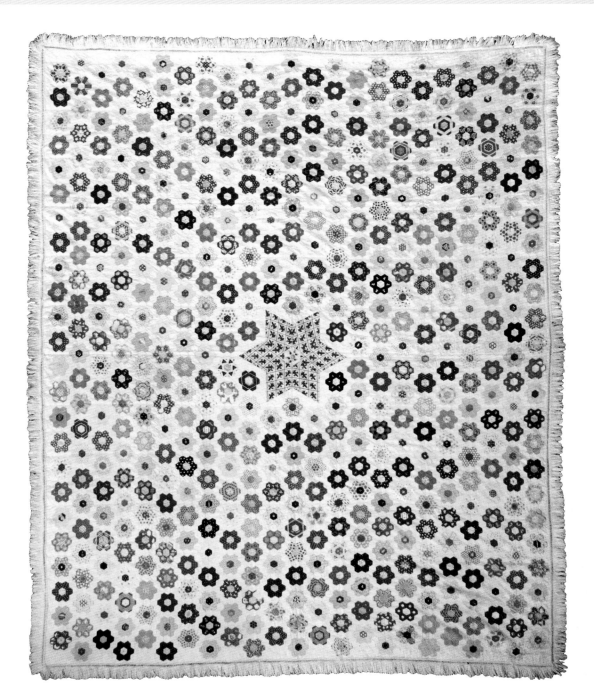

"Honeycomb," circa 1810–1830, 98" x 82". Maker unknown. From the collection of the Shelburne Museum. Photo courtesy of the Shelburne Museum, Shelburne, Vermont.

Look at this: We imagine that the early-nineteenth-century maker of this quilt did not have the aid of a see-through template to help her fussy cut the hundreds of pieces. Nevertheless, she managed to create wonderful secondary patterns that dazzle the eye in this visually stunning and beautifully pieced quilt.

19

"Flying Geese Medallion," circa 1860–1880, 79" x 79".
Made by a member of the Brush family, Cambridge, Vermont. From the collection of the
Shelburne Museum. Photo courtesy of the Shelburne Museum, Shelburne, Vermont.

Look at this: This skillfully pieced quilt was an exercise in time and patience. In her efforts to make sure that the flying-geese and half-square-triangle rows would fit without the need to "chop off the ends," the quiltmaker introduced solid strips of various widths between border rounds of pieced blocks to cope with the size differences. Directional changes in the flying-geese units, gutsy color choices, and strategic placement of striped and directional prints give this quilt lots of visual interest, movement, and depth.

*"Sugar Loaf Quilt," circa 1880, 78" x 74". New England maker unknown.
From the collection of Fumie Ono. (Detail on page 14.)*

Look at this: This quiltmaker displayed incredible accuracy in piecing the tiny 1" x 1½" diamonds into pyramids. We love her fearless use of color in her unusual and bold combination of madder (reddish brown), cheddar (orange), and pink, with just a hint of bouncy light blue.

By the way, have you ever wondered how some quilt blocks got their names? Perhaps this one relates to the block's resemblance to a sugarloaf, the tall, cylindrical, tapering cone shape that sugar was shipped in during the era this quilt was made. "Sugar pliers" made of iron were used to chip off bits of sugar to hold between the teeth as a person sipped his or her tea.

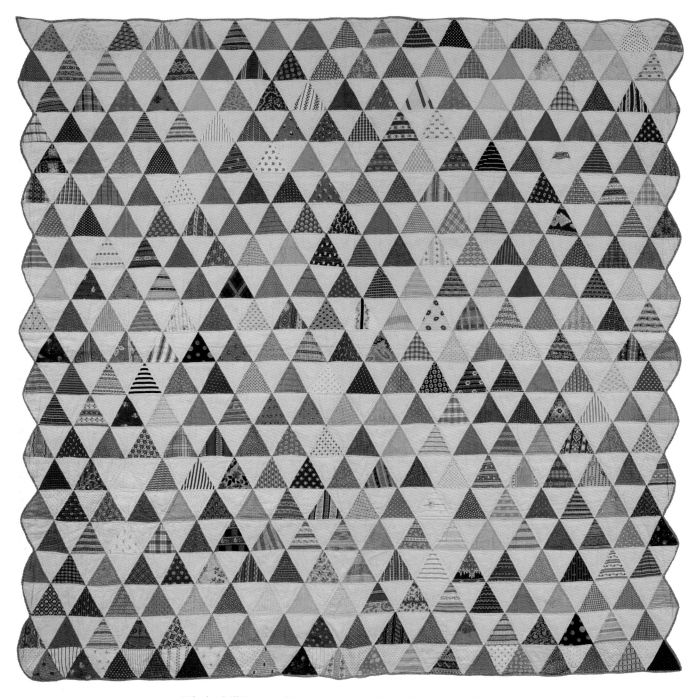

"Shakerhill Pyramid," circa 1890, 77" x 74". Maker unknown.
From the collection of Biz Storms.

Look at this: This One Patch Charm quilt (after innumerable hours of study, we found only one fabric that repeats) is stitched in the pyramid pattern and echo quilted. Note the interesting border treatment; the top and bottom are bound straight, while the sides are bound following the pyramid design, causing the scallops to be offset from side to side. We find little quirks like these are what give a quilt its personality and interest.

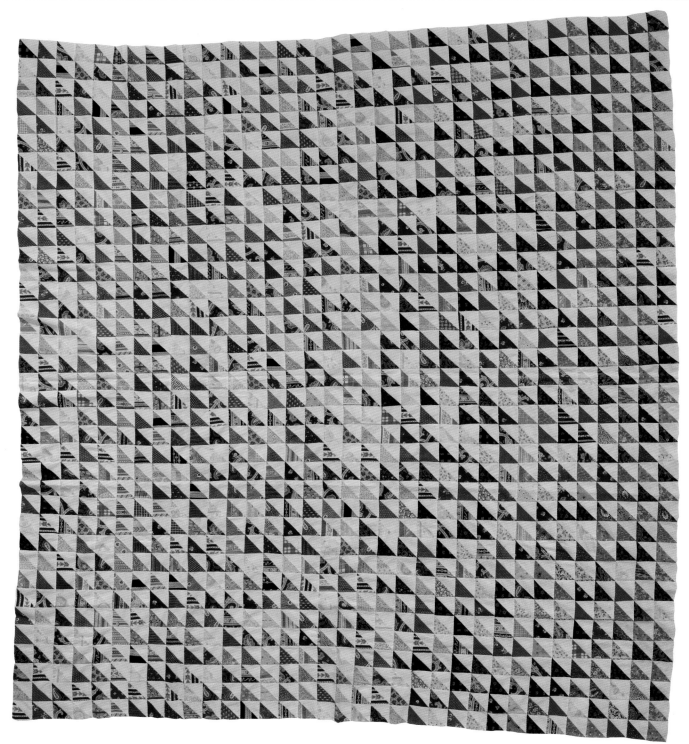

*"Martha's Vineyard," circa 1870, 74" x 80". Maker unknown.
From the collection of Biz Storms. (Detail on page 11.)*

Look at this: This top was Biz's first antique quilt purchase.
She was drawn by the simplicity of the design and the astounding array of fabric. Despite the hundreds of tiny half-square-triangle blocks, the skillful quiltmaker kept this quilt from exerting visual overload by pairing muslin with the dozens and dozens of different prints.

23

"Rajah Quilt," circa 1841, 127" x 132". Made by British women prisoners on board the convict ship, Rajah.
From the collection of the National Gallery of Australia, Canberra. Gift of Les Hollings and the Australian Textiles Fund 1989.

Look at this: This pieced, medallion-style, unlined coverlet has a center worked in *broderie perse* (motifs cut whole from a printed fabric, often chintz, and used as appliqués) that is surrounded by multiple "frames," including appliquéd borders, pieced borders, and strips of printed cloth. It contains 2,815 pieces, and it is a virtual library of period fabrics. If you look carefully, you'll find many instances where the quiltmakers cut the blocks short to make a row fit.

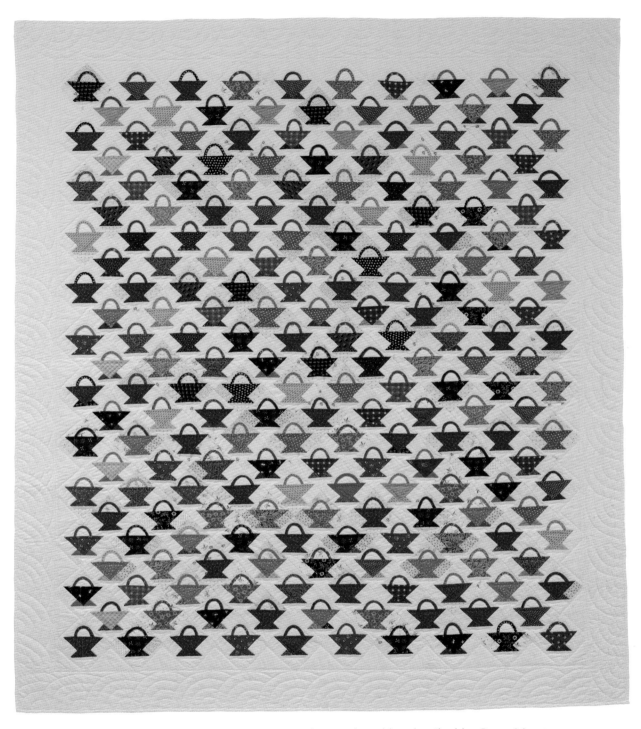

"Little Baskets," 2006, 64" x 74". Designed, pieced, and hand quilted by Gwen Marston, Beaver Island, Michigan. From the collection of Gwen Marston. (Detail on page 9.)

Look at this: Although not an antique, this cheerful and spirited small-block quilt by Gwen Marston definitely makes our hearts sing! It was a big hit at Gwen's 2007 Beaver Island Quilt Retreat, where the focus was on basket designs. Here the little pieced baskets line up in vertical, horizontal, and diagonal rows, creating a sense of order that is in joyous contrast to the machine-appliquéd handles worked in the quiltmaker's trademark liberated style. This quilt truly embodies Gwen's attitude toward quilt design, embracing the tradition and history of the art while adding her own touch of whimsy.

25

Big Lessons from (and for) Small Blocks

Here are some valuable lessons to guide you on your small-block adventure.

Lesson 1: Let Loose and Play

We cannot stress enough the value of play to loosen the artistic spirit. Make some experimental blocks. Yes, cut into some of your "good fabric" and try out different color combinations. Stretch your creativity. Sewing techniques should be well executed and tidy. That being said, mistakes happen. That's okay. We call this "charm" in a quilt! You can save your playing blocks for a "sampler quilt." Imagine snuggling under all of that creative energy!

Lesson 2: Do Your Homework

Study old quilts. With lots and lots of exposure to them, you will find over time that you are taking in loads of information about their design and color. Pick one of your favorites and copy it as faithfully as possible. The lessons are plentiful. You'll notice that

Detail of "Leap of Faith." The title of this quilt is most appropriate, as Mary Elizabeth employed some of the free-spirited techniques (including cutting off border strips to make them fit) that appear so often in antique quilts. For a full view (and instructions), see page 66.

Enhance the visual interest of your quilt by introducing directional prints and prints with motifs in various sizes.

Don't be afraid to toss a few "shockers" into the mix. You'll be surprised at the personality they bring to your small-block quilts.

these quilts often bear witness to the saying "necessity is the mother of invention," and we encourage you to "invent" as the situation demands. If it's too long, cut it off. If it's too short, add some on. If you run out of one fabric, find a mate and stitch the two fabrics together to get the length you need or cut the remaining pieces you need to complete the block.

Lesson 3: Choose Appropriate Materials

As for the "nuts and bolts," we use 100%-cotton fabric, which we do not prewash. Variety is the key. Look for fabrics with prints of different scale. When cut up into small pieces, these fabrics can drop surprising bits of color into your work to add visual interest. Directional prints are also great for creating movement. We have found that there are often more woven homespuns than you might think in antique quilts, and we love adding them to our quilts. And of course, when choosing the fabrics for your project, don't forget the "shockers," which can spark some wonderful color combinations. Shockers are those fabrics that make you cringe when you look at them but that can add magic to your quilt.

While we both like to approach our quilting from an intuitive and relaxed perspective, with small-block quilts, precise measuring, cutting, and seam allowances are essential. To maximize your cutting accuracy, use the lines on your ruler and not the ones on your cutting board. A nonslip sheet or small sandpaper stickers applied to the backs of your rulers will help "grip" the fabric and help with accuracy too.

Sew with good quality, 100%-cotton thread using the same thread on the top and in the bobbin. In blocks this small, different thickness or plies can affect the accuracy of your piecing. A sample block will help you take this factor into account.

Lesson 4: Make a Sample Block

Unless the directions state otherwise, sew with a scant ¼" seam allowance. The tiny extra bit of fabric is taken up when the pieced unit is opened and the seam allowance is pressed. Taking the time to verify your measurements, cuts, and seam allowances in a sample block helps ensure that the quilt top will piece together smoothly. A deviation of ¹⁄₁₆" on a block can multiply quickly across a quilt top and, before you know it, become a difference of an inch or two!

Pay special attention when pressing, using a light up-and-down motion (no ironing back and forth) to avoid pulling the pieces out of shape.

Lesson 5: Take Time to Smell the Roses

We have chosen to adopt some of the more traditional ways of piecing our small blocks. While lots of the projects listed would work with strip piecing and faster production methods (which you can certainly use if you like), we prefer the meditative quality of seeing a block, or two, or three develop before our eyes. We think of it as the Zen of quilting . . . slowing down enough to enjoy the process and the fabrics.

This doesn't mean that we shun efficiency. With each project in this book, you'll find a section called "Batch Work" which includes information about cutting, assembling the blocks, and/or putting the quilt top together in manageable "chunks" or "batches"—extremely useful when making a quilt with lots and lots of blocks and pieces! Many of these recommendations involve chain piecing, a time- and thread-saving technique (see box at right). For added efficiency, we use one-layer tackle boxes with dividers to organize and store small pieces. They also make the pieces easy to transport and nice and accessible for batch work.

And remember, chocolate helps!

A tackle box with dividers is one of our favorite tools for keeping things organized. The chocolate is for . . . well, chocolate!

CHAIN PIECE FOR EFFICIENCY

Chain piecing is an efficient method of sewing together like pieces, units, and rows—a valuable technique to have in your repertoire when making small-block quilts.

1. Place the pieces you wish to assemble beside you at your sewing machine. Sometimes these will already be right sides together and paired for sewing; sometimes you will be working from separate stacks and pairing as you go.

2. Sew the first pair of pieces from cut edge to cut edge. At the end of the seam, stop sewing, but *do not cut the thread.*

3. Feed the next pair of pieces under the presser foot, and stitch them together. Continue feeding pieces through the machine without cutting the threads in between. You do not need to backstitch since seams typically will be crossed and secured by later seams.

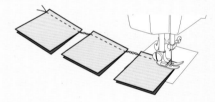

4. When all the pieces in the batch have been sewn, remove the chain from the machine and cut the ending thread. In some cases you will immediately clip the threads between the pieces; in some cases you will leave the connecting threads intact and begin another round of chain piecing. The individual project instructions will guide you.

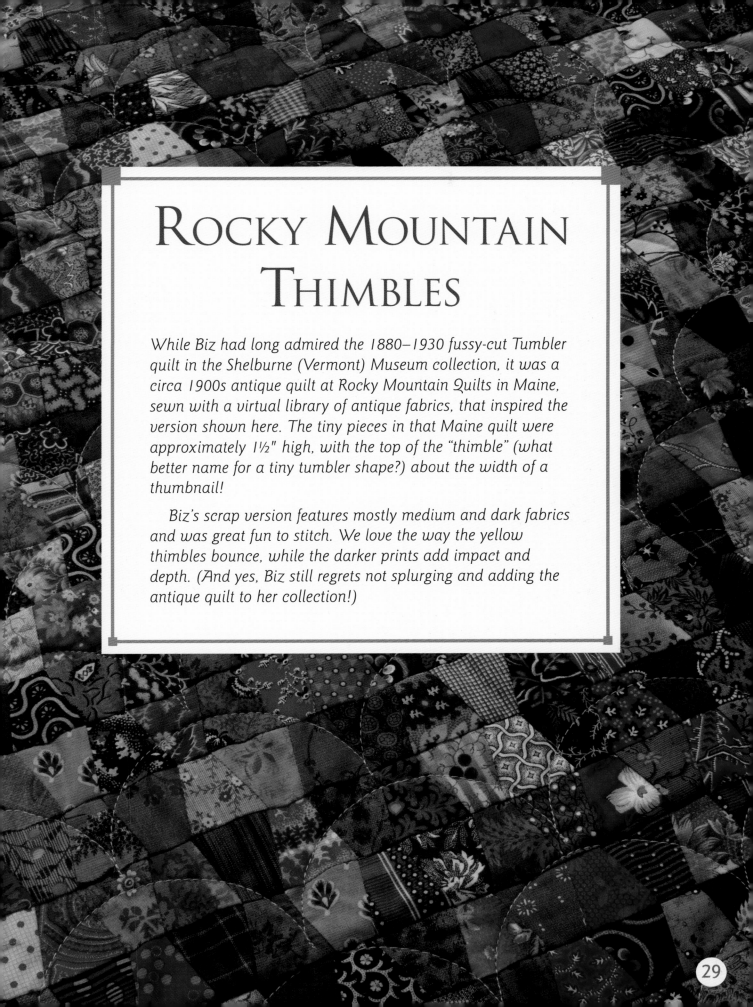

ROCKY MOUNTAIN THIMBLES

While Biz had long admired the 1880–1930 fussy-cut Tumbler quilt in the Shelburne (Vermont) Museum collection, it was a circa 1900s antique quilt at Rocky Mountain Quilts in Maine, sewn with a virtual library of antique fabrics, that inspired the version shown here. The tiny pieces in that Maine quilt were approximately 1½" high, with the top of the "thimble" (what better name for a tiny tumbler shape?) about the width of a thumbnail!

Biz's scrap version features mostly medium and dark fabrics and was great fun to stitch. We love the way the yellow thimbles bounce, while the darker prints add impact and depth. (And yes, Biz still regrets not splurging and adding the antique quilt to her collection!)

Pieced by Biz Storms, Toronto, Canada, 2007.
Machine quilted by Sandra Reed. Detail on page 16.

Finished Quilt: 76" x 95½"

Materials

All yardages are based on 42"- wide fabric.

14 yards *total* of assorted medium and dark prints for thimble shapes

1 yard of fabric for binding

7 yards of fabric for backing

84" x 103" piece of batting

Small piece of sandpaper or cardboard for template

Cutting

See "Cutting the Thimbles" at right for an efficient method to rotary cut the thimble shapes. Cut all strips across the fabric width (selvage to selvage).

From the binding fabric, cut:

10 strips, 2¾" x 42"

QUILT ON THE GO

Thimble units are perfect for hand stitching into rows. Toss a handful of units, needle, thread, scissors, and thimble into a pencil case, and you've got a portable project. This is also a great project for a young quilter as a row stitches up quickly and easily.

Cutting the Thimbles

"Rocky Mountain Thimbles" includes a total of 6,536 thimble shapes, arranged in 76 horizontal rows of thimbles, with 86 thimbles in each row. While it sounds like a lot, you can rotary cut them quite quickly.

1. Cut the assorted medium and dark prints into 1¾"-wide strips. Stack them several layers high, carefully aligning the edges.

2. Use the thimble pattern on page 33 to make a template from sandpaper or cardboard. Using the template as a guide, rotary cut thimble shapes along the length of the layered strips, rotating the template 180° between each cut.

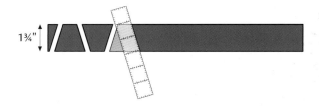

1¾"

3. Continue layering strips and cutting thimbles until you have cut a total of 6,536 thimble shapes.

Actual size

31

Batch Work

Once you've cut the required number of thimbles, you can start preparing sets of 86 shapes, enough to stitch into a horizontal row. Refer to "Chain Piece for Efficiency" on page 28 as needed.

1. Toss the thimble shapes into a large container and mix them up. Count out 86 random pieces and store them in a resealable container, such as a snack-sized plastic bag. Continue counting and storing until you have a total of 76 separate containers with 86 pieces in each.

TAKE A BREAK!

If you'd like, alternate between cutting thimble shapes (individually or from strips) and sorting them into sets to break up the task of cutting so many pieces. Ask a youngster to help with the sorting. It's a fun assignment for kids, and they get to practice their counting skills!

---

2. Remove the thimble shapes from six sorted thimble containers and stack them side by side beside your sewing machine.

3. With right sides together, matching the narrow top of one piece with the wider bottom of the other, sew two thimbles from stack 1 together as shown.

4. Without cutting the thread, take two thimbles from stack 2 and sew them together, reversing the top and bottom orientation as shown so the narrow ends and wide ends line up with the previous pair. Repeat to make a pair with two thimbles from stack 3, and then stack 4, stack 5, and stack 6. Cut the chain loose from the machine after sewing the last pair, but *do not cut the pairs apart.*

5. Continue chain piecing to add a third, fourth, fifth thimble (and so on) from each stack until you have completed six horizontal rows of 86 pieces each. (You will have no thimbles left in any of the original six stacks.) Press the seam allowances in alternating directions from row to row, but *do not cut the connecting threads.*

6. With right sides together, sew the rows together as shown, carefully butting the seam allowances; press. Wide and narrow ends should align with like ends.

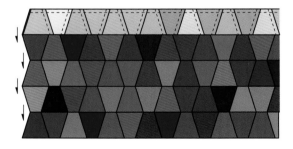

CALL IT CHARM!

Despite the abundance of fabrics used, you will occasionally find thimbles of the same fabric adjacent to one another. We call this "charm," and enjoy this happy accident when it occurs.

---

7. Repeat steps 2–6 to make a total of 12 six-row units and one four-row unit.

Quilt Assembly and Finishing

Refer to "Finishing School" (page 84) for guidance as needed with the following steps.

1. Referring to the assembly diagram below, arrange and sew the units together as shown; press.

2. Use a rotary cutter and long ruler to trim and straighten the left and right edges of the quilt.

3. Layer, baste, and quilt your quilt. (Sandra quilted a simple overall clamshell pattern to complement the quilt's one-patch design.) Use the 2¾"-wide strips to make and attach a double-fold binding, and don't forget to add a label.

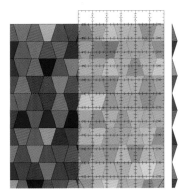

Trim.

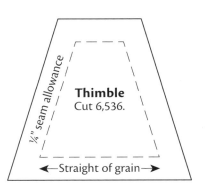

¼" seam allowance

Thimble
Cut 6,536.

←Straight of grain→

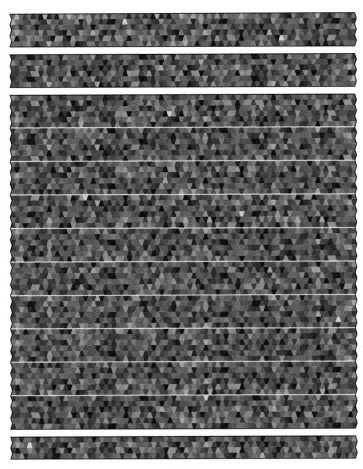

Assembly diagram

VILLAGE QUILT

They say it takes a village to raise a child, and it surely took a village to make this quilt, inspired by an 1830 quilt in the Shelburne Museum collection (see page 19). The original, in shades of muted blues, browns, and pinks, formed secondary patterns with its mesmerizing fussy-cut hexagons.

For her version, which we chose to paper piece for accuracy, Mary Elizabeth selected a palette of saturated dark to medium blues, purples, blackish browns, browns, and reds for the outer rings or petals, letting their rich tones contrast with the pale centers she chose to complement the muslin paths between each "floret." Many of the petal fabrics have small "highlights" of color that add life to the quilt: bits of orange in a flower or the smidge of green in a leaf. Not all the fabrics are bright and bold prints; some sedate prints add needed balance to quiet the quilt.

Warning: These little paper-pieced florets are highly addictive. Create this quilt at your own risk. No 12-step program is currently available, and withdrawal can be severe!

Finished Size: 60½" x 82⅞"
Block Count: 152

Materials

All yardages are based on 42"- wide fabric.

3⅛ yards of muslin for garden paths

2⅞ yards *total* of assorted medium-dark to dark red, blue, purple, brown, and black prints for floret petals*

2⅝ yards of dark fabric for border

½ yard *total* of assorted light prints for floret centers*

¾ yard of fabric for binding

5⅛ yards of fabric for backing

68" x 91" piece of batting

¾" Paper Pieces paper hexagons**

Small piece of sandpaper, cardboard, or see-through template material

If you plan to fussy cut (page 38), you may need additional fabric.

**These come in packages of 750 and 1,500. You will need approximately 2,000 paper hexagons for this project. Paper hexagons are reusable. See "Resources" on page 92. If you prefer to make your own paper templates, use the pattern on page 40.*

Cutting

See "Cutting the Hexagons" on page 37 for information on cutting the hexagons. Cut all strips across the fabric width (selvage to selvage) unless otherwise noted.

From the muslin, cut:

51 strips, 1⅞" x 42"; crosscut into 966 pieces, 2" x 1⅞".

From the *lengthwise grain* of the border fabric, cut:

2 strips, 8" x 45½"

2 strips, 8" x 82⅞"

From the binding fabric, cut:

8 strips, 2¾" x 42"

Actual size

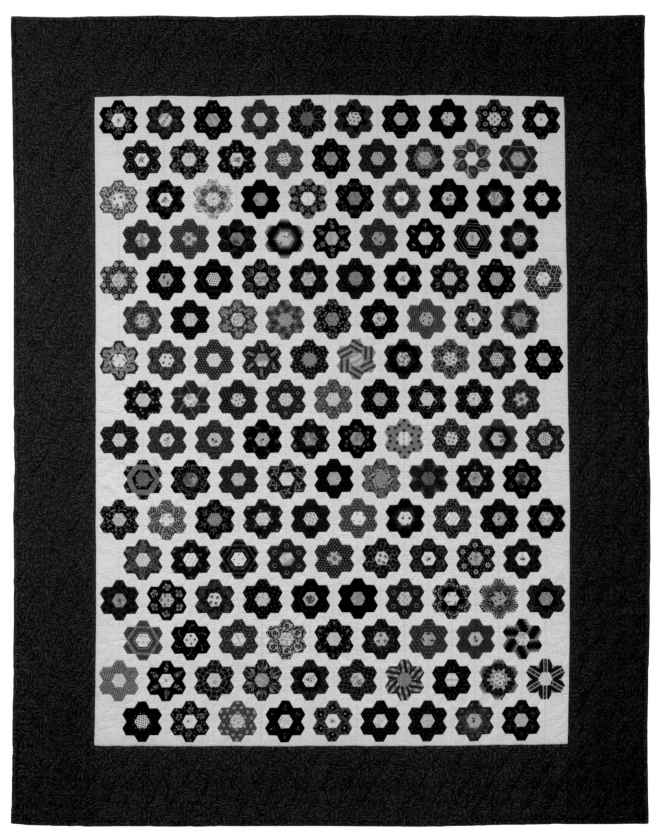

Pieced by Mary Elizabeth Kinch, Biz Storms, Amberlea Williams, Kathy Albino,
Catherine Schuler, Judy Ellen, Jennifer Purcell-Martin, and Myrna Atangan,
Toronto, Canada, 2007. Hand quilted by Mary Elizabeth Kinch. Detail on page 38.

Cutting the Hexagons

"Village Quilt" includes a garden path made from 828 muslin hexagons (A), 38 muslin half hexagons (B), 96 muslin half hexagons (C), and four muslin quarter hexagons (D). While it sounds like a lot, you can rotary cut them quite quickly. Mary Elizabeth fussy cut both the floret petals and the centers to create interesting secondary designs. For more on fussy cutting, see "Fantastic Fussy Cuts" on page 38.

1. Place a hexagon paper template in the center of a 2" x 1⅞" piece of muslin, taking care with the grain-line placement as shown. Pin, and then cut out the shape, leaving a ¼" seam allowance all around. Cut 828 hexagons and label them piece A.

Piece A.
Cut 828.

2. Cut 19 hexagon papers in half as shown to make 38 half-hexagon templates. Center a template on a 2" x 1⅞" piece of muslin, taking care with the grain-line placement. Pin, and then cut out the shape, leaving a ¼" seam allowance all around. Cut 38 half hexagons and label them piece B.

Cut 19 templates in half.

Piece B.
Cut 38.

3. Cut 48 hexagon papers in half in the opposite direction as shown to make 96 half-hexagon templates. Center a template on a 2" x 1⅞" piece of muslin, taking care with the grain-line placement.

Pin, and then cut out the shape, leaving a ¼" seam allowance all around. Cut 96 half hexagons and label them piece C.

Cut 48 templates in half.

Piece C.
Cut 96.

4. Cut one hexagon paper into quarters as shown to make four quarter-hexagon templates for corner pieces. Center a template on a 2" x 1⅞" piece of muslin, taking care with the grain-line placement. Pin, and then cut out the shape, leaving a ¼" seam allowance all around.

Cut 1 template in quarters.

Piece D.
Cut 4.

5. For the petals, place a hexagon paper template on the wrong side of an assorted medium-dark to dark print. Pin, and then cut out the shape, leaving a ¼" seam allowance all around. Cut 912 hexagons in matching sets of six. You may need to ignore the grain line if you fussy cut the petals.

6. For the floret centers, repeat step 5 to cut a total of 152 hexagons from the assorted light prints. These do not need to be in matching sets.

Batch Work

You can easily baste the hexagons for the muslin paths in batches. Mary Elizabeth also fussy cut the florets in batches, basted them, and then attached each center in the batch to its petals before cutting the next batch. If you like, you can then attach the florets together in rows by piecing with one basted muslin piece between each floret as described in "Quilt Top Assembly and Finishing," steps 1 and 2 on page 39. A thimble is helpful to protect your fingers when basting and assembling the hexagon pieces.

FANTASTIC FUSSY CUTS

When cutting the florets, Mary Elizabeth paid special attention to any secondary patterns that might form in adjoining petals when the pieces were sewn together. We never ceased to be amazed by what the fabric showed us. Large prints, small prints, floral patterns, circles, and dots each created their own unique bursts of pattern. Directional fabrics were particularly surprising in the spinning patterns that evolved. The same fabric would often give a totally different look in two different florets.

A detail of "Village Quilt" shows some of the wonderful effects possible when you fussy cut the petals.

If you want to create a secondary pattern in your florets by fussy cutting, accurate placement of the paper hexagon piece is a must. (Mary Elizabeth found it helpful to create a template from see-through plastic template material that included the seam allowance to help with the placing and cutting. You may also find a light box can be very helpful in assessing accurate placement of the paper piece on the fabric.) Choose a landmark on the print for placement, mark and position the paper piece consistently for all six petals, pin, and cut. Place a piece of 200-grade fine sandpaper underneath your fabric so it doesn't slip as you trace.

Assembling the Florets

1. For each floret, begin with a light print (center) hexagon. Working one side at a time, fold the edges of the fabric over the edges of the paper and baste in place with a running stitch through all three layers. Check your work as you go to ensure that there is no pulling or distortion of the print. Repeat to baste six matching medium-dark or dark print hexagons for the petals.

2. Arrange the six matching hexagons (petals) around the light hexagon (center) to form a floret. Place one petal right sides together with the center piece. Starting with two stitches in the corner, sew the common side together with small stitches in matching or blending thread, taking a good bite of fabric from each edge. When you reach the corner, take two stitches in place to secure. Do not break or tie off the thread.

3. Open the two pieces that you sewed together in step 2. Check to see that the stitches are tight enough that when you hold the unit up to the light, you do not see light coming through the seam. Your stitches should be almost invisible.

4. Place the next petal right sides together with the center, and continuing with the same thread, sew the two pieces together, again starting and ending with two anchoring stitches. Continue in this manner until all six petals have been sewn to the

center. Use the same method to stitch the seams between each petal.

5. Repeat steps 1–4 to make 152 florets.

Preparing the Muslin Pieces

Baste each muslin hexagon, half hexagon, and quarter hexagon to the appropriate template as described in step 1 of "Assembling the Florets." Do not baste over the inside edges of the half and quarter hexagons, as these edges will be the seam allowance for attaching the border.

Quilt Top Assembly and Finishing

Refer to "Finishing School" (page 84) for guidance as needed with the following steps.

1. Referring to the assembly diagram on page 40, lay out 10 florets and nine basted muslin hexagons (A), alternating them as shown. Paper piece two sides of each A piece to the two adjacent florets as described in "Assembling the Florets." Make eight rows.

2. Repeat step 1 using nine florets and 10 A hexagons. Make eight rows.

3. Still referring to the assembly diagram, arrange the rows from steps 1 and 2 on your design wall, alternating them as shown. Fill in between the rows with basted muslin hexagons (A). Paper piece the hexagons into rows, and then paper piece the hexagon and floret rows together.

4. Fill in the edges of the quilt top with basted muslin hexagons (A), half-hexagons (B and C), and quarter-hexagon (D) and paper piece to complete the quilt top. Remove the basting and papers from all pieces.

5. With right sides together, sew the 8" x 45½" dark borders to the top and bottom of the quilt. Press the seam allowances toward the borders. Sew the 8" x 82⅞" dark borders to the sides; press.

6. Layer, baste, and quilt your quilt. (Mary Elizabeth quilted the center area of the quilt in a simple vertical-line pattern to minimize the number of seams she would cross and to balance the circular pattern of the florets. She quilted the borders with diagonal lines using the angles of the hexagons as guideposts.) Use the 2¾"-wide strips to make and attach a double-fold binding, and don't forget to add a label.

Assembly diagram

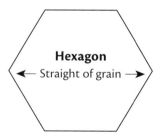

Quilt plan

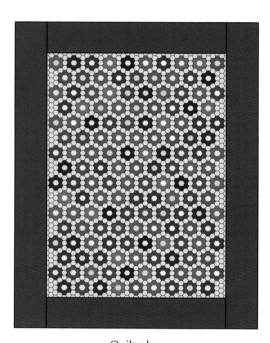

Hexagon
← Straight of grain →

Note: Respect grain line when possible.

KATHY'S QUILT

Our love affair with ½" finished squares or 1½" finished Nine Patch blocks goes back to our friend, Kathy Metelica, who nonchalantly mentioned that we might like to have a peek at her latest acquisition, a circa 1860 Nine Patch Postage Stamp quilt. We truly lost the ability to speak and reminded each other that breathing was a good thing.

This quilt set the gold standard for us for anything that features a Nine Patch block. We've since spent many hours pouring over the thousands of postage-stamp-sized pieces in that astounding scrap quilt and have made some surprising discoveries. Fabrics that we'd previously considered "shockers"—that is teeth-gritting, only-a-mother-could-love ugly—were the very fabrics that added that special zing. We've found the same is true with some of the odd colors, the kinds of things that we'd passed by before, usually in the remnants bin. Finally, to our amazement, the quilt contained a considerable number of homespun fabrics. We now perceive the reliable Nine Patch in a totally different light!

For her quilt, Biz wanted the quiet purple, gray, and black prints to get some attention. She paired them with a high-energy shirting print (white- or ecru-based prints with tiny figures in blacks, browns, navy blues, and so on) and was tickled with the results. This is a quilt that crackles, which speaks wonders for the simple Nine Patch block.

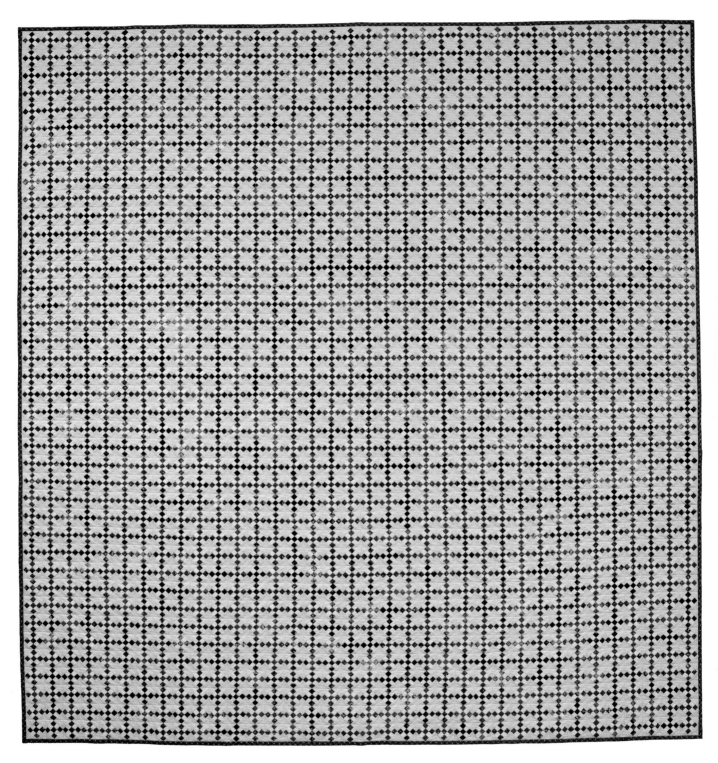

Pieced by Biz Storms, Toronto, Canada, 2007.
Machine quilted by Margaret Mitchell. Detail on page 11.

Finished Quilt: 76⅞" x 85½"
Finished Block: 1½" x 1½"
Block Count: 1,440

Materials

All yardages are based on 42"-wide fabric.

5½ yards *total* of assorted dark prints for blocks

4⅝ yards of light print for alternate squares and
    setting triangles

4½ yards of muslin for blocks

⅞ yard of fabric for binding

7⅛ yards of fabric for backing (with horizontal seams)

85" x 93" piece of batting

PLEASURE SQUARED

The Nine Patch blocks for this quilt are pieced
using individual 1" squares rather than strip
piecing, which is admittedly faster. However, our
method is more accommodating for working with
lots of fabrics in smaller quantities and, for us,
it is simply a more enjoyable way to work. On
a practical note, the blocks lend themselves to
hand piecing as a take-along project.

Cutting

Cut all strips across the fabric width (selvage to selvage).

From the assorted dark prints, cut a *total of*:

7,200 squares, 1" x 1", in matching sets of 5

From the muslin, cut:

148 strips, 1" x 42"; crosscut into 5,760 squares, 1" x 1"

From the light print, cut:

72 strips, 2" x 42"; crosscut into 1,365 squares, 2" x 2"

4 strips, 3⅜" x 42"; crosscut into 37 squares, 3⅜" x 3⅜".
    Cut each square twice diagonally to yield 148
    quarter-square triangles.

2 squares, 3" x 3"; cut each square once diagonally to
    yield 4 half-square triangles

From the binding fabric, cut:

9 strips, 2¾" x 42"

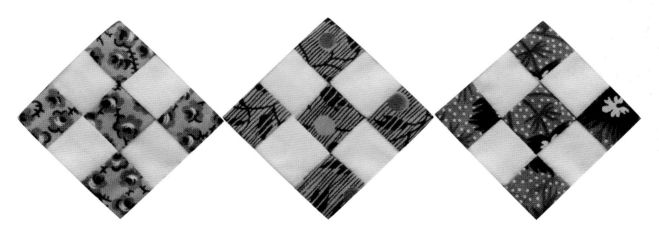

Actual size

Batch Work

Here's a great way to sew batches of 25 Nine Patch blocks. You will need 125 dark 1" squares in matching sets of five and 100 muslin 1" squares. Refer to "Chain Piece for Efficiency" on page 28 as needed.

1. Divide the 125 dark squares into five stacks of 25 squares each, with one square of each fabric in each stack. Be sure to keep the fabric order the same in all the stacks. Label the stacks from 1 through 5. Set aside stacks 4 and 5, placing each in a resealable snack bag or small container. Set stacks 1–3 and the muslin squares beside your sewing machine as shown.

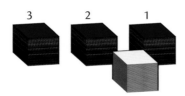

2. With right sides together, sew the top dark square from stack 1 to a muslin square. Without cutting the thread, sew the next dark square from stack 1 to the next muslin square. Repeat until you have chain pieced each dark square from stack 1 to a muslin square.

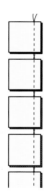

3. Without cutting the threads, continue chain piecing, substituting the dark squares from stack 2 for the stack 1 squares. Repeat using the stack 3 squares. You will now have a total of 75 pairs on the chain. Cut the chain loose after sewing the last pair, but *do not cut the pairs apart*.

4. Retrieve stacks 4 and 5 and place them beside your sewing machine with the remaining muslin squares. Sew the top dark square from stack 4 to the opposite side of the muslin square that begins the chain you completed in step 3. (The dark squares should match.) Without cutting the thread, sew the next dark square from stack 4 to the next muslin square. Repeat until you have chain pieced each dark square from stack 4, and then stack 5, to the chain.

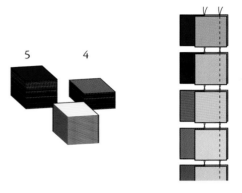

5. Cut the threads between each dark/muslin/dark unit, leaving the rest of the chain intact. Press the seam allowances toward the dark squares.

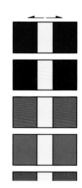

6. Resume chain piecing to stitch a muslin square to the opposite side of each dark square in the remaining chain. Cut the threads between each unit. Press the seam allowances toward the dark square.

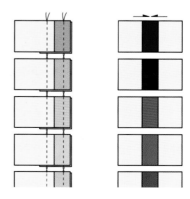

7. Arrange two matching units from step 5 and a matching unit from step 6 as shown. Stitch the units together; press. Make 25 Nine Patch blocks.

Make 25.

Nine patch as it appears stitched into the quilt.

8. Repeat steps 1–7 to make a total of 1,440 blocks.

Quilt Assembly and Finishing

Refer to "Finishing School" (page 84) for guidance as needed with the following steps.

1. Referring to the assembly diagram below, arrange the Nine Patch blocks, 2" light squares, quarter-square triangles, and half-square triangles into rows as shown.

2. Assemble the quilt in diagonal rows or using the technique described in "Setting Blocks on Point" (page 85). Press the seam allowances away from the Nine Patch blocks.

3. Layer, baste, and quilt your quilt. (Margaret quilted in an overall diagonal grid, with the diagonals crossing in the centers of the light squares.) Use the 2¾"-wide strips to make and attach a double-fold binding, and don't forget to add a label.

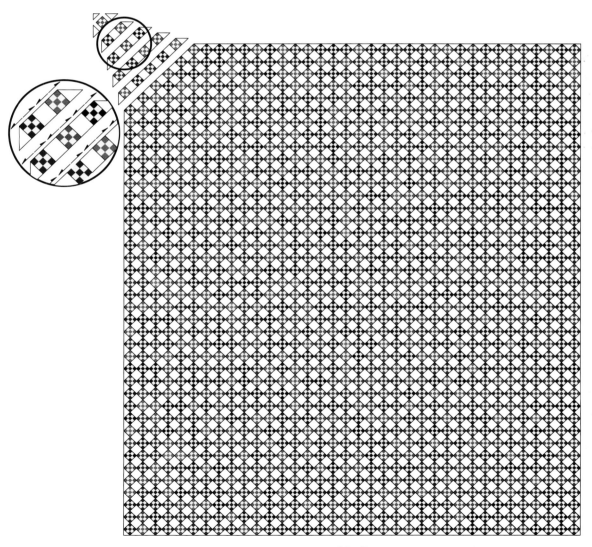

Assembly diagram

FARMHOUSE QUILT

Making this quilt is playing with fabric at its relaxing best! It was inspired by many antique examples we've seen. (We love them even when they're faded and worn.) In this version, Mary Elizabeth wanted to explore both random design and a scrappy look in a palette that included mostly blues, browns, and shirtings. She tossed in a tiny bit of green and purple to add some zip.

By using our random-batching technique, we were able to put this quilt together quickly and easily. The wide variety of fabrics, colors, and value contrasts made it possible to sew the blocks together randomly without "art directing" as we sewed. Try it! The batches swiftly turn into rows, making this a quilt you can work on in stages, as time permits.

Finished Size: 70½" x 91½"
Finished Block: 3½" x 3½"
Block Count: 520

Materials

All yardages are based on 42"- wide fabric. While the yardage listed below is total yardage needed, purchasing quarter yards, fat quarters (18" x 22"), and even fat eighths (9" x 22") will help you acquire the assortment of colors and values you'll need for this quilt.

11 yards *total* of assorted brown, blue, shirting, green, and purple prints for blocks*

⅞ yard of fabric for binding

5⅝ yards of fabric for backing

78" x 98" piece of batting

We aimed for a fabric mix of roughly 30% browns, 30% blues, 20% shirtings, 15% purples, and 5% greens.

Cutting

Cut all strips across the fabric width (selvage to selvage).

Before we began cutting, we set some loose design parameters. For our blocks, we wanted the corner squares and the side rectangles of each block to be contrasting values and each corner square and side rectangle in the block to be cut from a different fabric. Then of course we proceeded to break our own rules! Remember: You are always free to make your own design decisions. Have fun—and play!

From the assorted brown, blue, shirting, green, and purple prints, cut *a total of:*

520 squares, 2½" x 2½"

2,080 squares, 1¼" x 1¼"

2,080 rectangles, 1¼" x 2½"

From the binding fabric, cut:

9 strips, 2¾" x 42"

Actual size

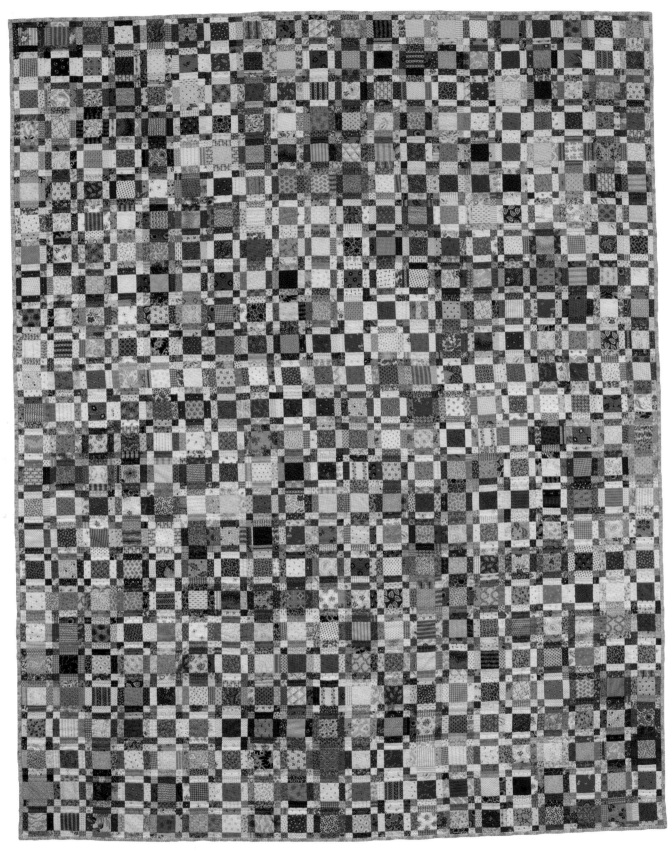

*Pieced and hand quilted by Mary Elizabeth Kinch and Biz Storms,
Toronto, Canada, 2007. Detail on page 17.*

Batch Work

This batch-work method is much more fun than the usual assembly-line technique; it's full of surprises! Try it to make a 26-block vertical row in a single sitting. How efficient is that? Refer to "Chain Piece for Efficiency" on page 28 as needed.

1. Randomly select twenty 2½" center squares and lay them out individually on a flat surface. Next, place a set of four 1¼" corner squares and then four 1¼" x 2½" side rectangles on top of each block center. Don't be too worried about adhering to any rules; just relax and deal out the fabrics like a deck of cards.

2. After selecting fabrics for the first 20 blocks, randomly deal out fabric pieces for the next 20 blocks, placing a set on top of each of your original stacks—no peeking allowed!

3. Continue making sets of pieces for 20 blocks, stacking a block on top of each of your previous stacks until all the pieces are gone. You will now have 20 stacks, each with enough fabric pieces to make 26 blocks—a vertical row.

4. Take one stack to your sewing machine and arrange the pieces for the first block. With right sides together, chain piece the pieces in the right-hand row to the pieces in the center row as shown. Do not cut the thread. Layer the remaining two corner squares and the side rectangle from the first block in sewing order (square, rectangle, square) and set them aside. They'll be added to the block after all 26 blocks in the batch have been partially assembled.

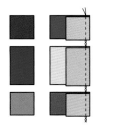

5. Arrange the pieces for the next block in the stack and chain piece as described in step 4. Layer the remaining pieces and place them on top of the remaining pieces for block 1. Continue arranging, chain piecing, and layering until you have finished the last block in the stack. Cut the chain loose after sewing the last pair, but *do not cut the pairs apart*.

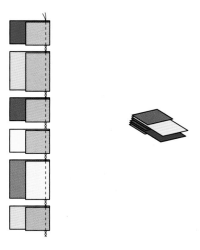

6. Rotate the chain so you are starting at the bottom of the row you finished in step 5. Working from the top of the stack of set-aside pieces, chain piece a corner square or side rectangle to the opposite edge of each unit on the chain as shown; press. Cut the chain loose after sewing the last units, but *do not cut the units apart*. Finger-press the units as shown.

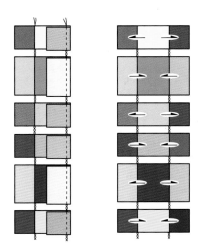

7. With right sides together, stitch the first, second, and third rows of the first block together as shown, carefully butting the seam allowances. Repeat to assemble the remaining blocks, stitching each to the previous block until the chain is complete. Trim any dangling threads and press the seam allowances in one direction. Label this row 1.

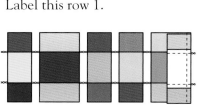

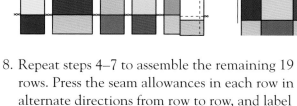

8. Repeat steps 4–7 to assemble the remaining 19 rows. Press the seam allowances in each row in alternate directions from row to row, and label them row 2, row 3, and so on.

Quilt Assembly and Finishing

Refer to "Finishing School" (page 84) for guidance as needed with the following steps.

1. Referring to the assembly diagram below, arrange the 20 vertical rows side by side as shown.

2. With right sides together, sew the vertical rows together, carefully butting the seam allowances; press.

3. Layer, baste, and quilt your quilt. (For the quilting, we freehand quilted a simple grid through the center of the corner squares and side rectangles to accentuate the block.) Use the 2¾"-wide strips to make and attach a double-fold binding, and don't forget to add a label.

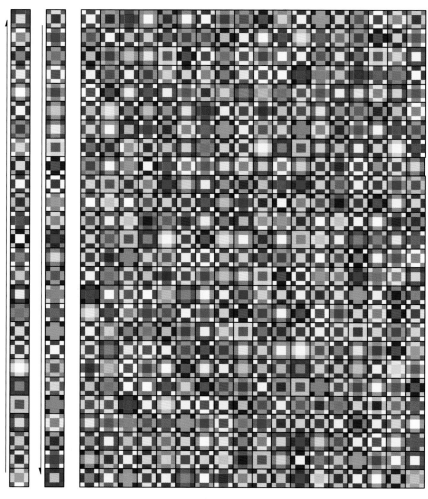

Assembly diagram

WHERE'S THE OTHER HALF?

We wanted to make a vibrant and joyous quilt with our chrome yellow and double-pink prints, and we also had been planning to make a quilt with blocks that consisted of half-square triangles. This lap quilt proved to be the perfect solution. We stitched a sample block with 1½" finished squares, but the half-square triangles looked way too podgy. Then we tried a block with ¾" finished squares, and the half-square triangles almost disappeared. The block with the 1" finished square was—as Goldilocks would say—"just right."

Most of the work for this quilt was completed at Mary Elizabeth's cottage, so we enjoyed a view of the lake as we stitched up all the yummy fabrics.

As for the title, we love this quilt so much, we've decided it just deserves to be larger. Perhaps someday . . .

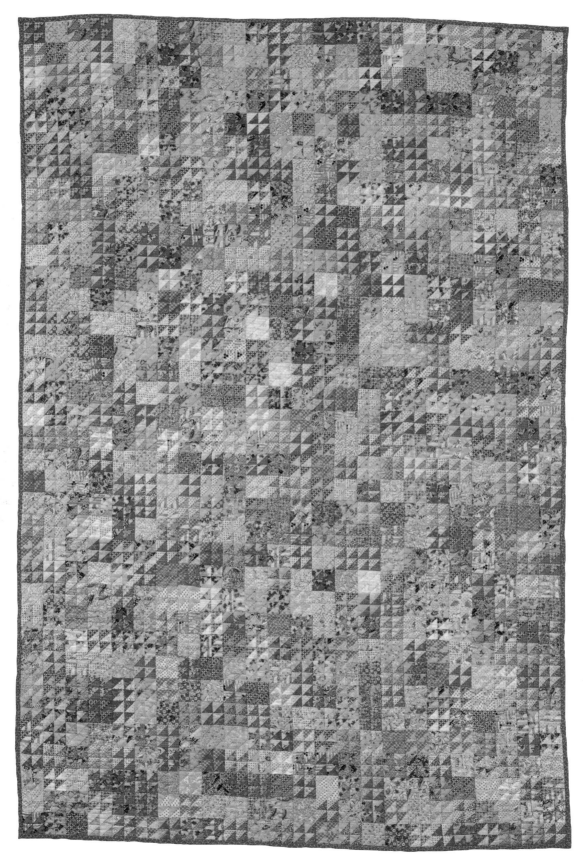

Pieced by Mary Elizabeth Kinch and Biz Storms,
Toronto, Canada, 2007. Hand quilted by Saloma Yoder.

Finished Size: 48½" x 72½"
Finished Block: 2" x 2"
Block Count: 864

Materials

All yardages are based on 42"-wide fabric.

5¾ yards *total* of assorted pink prints for blocks

5¾ yards *total* of assorted yellow prints for blocks

½ yard of binding fabric

3¼ yards of backing fabric (for horizontal seam)

56" x 80" piece of batting

MIX 'N' MATCH

We found we could create an impressive number of pink and yellow fabric combinations with the triangles for this quilt. Once everything was cut, we matched four triangles from each yellow print with four triangles from each pink print for as long as the yellow prints lasted. Then we switched up and started again.

Note that some squares deviate from the pink and yellow formula and contain two different pinks. (Just cut a few extra matching pairs.) This unpredictability makes the quilt more interesting and adds visual energy.

Cutting

Cut all strips across the fabric width (selvage to selvage).

From the assorted pink prints, cut *a total of*:

1,728 squares, 2" x 2", in matching pairs; cut each square once diagonally to yield 3,456 half-square triangles*

From the assorted yellow prints, cut *a total of*:

1,728 squares, 2" x 2", in matching pairs; cut each square once diagonally to yield 3,456 half-square triangles*

From the binding fabric, cut:

7 strips, 2¾" x 42"

*Rather than fuss with ⅛" measurements for the tiny half-square-triangle units, we opted to cut and halve 2" squares and sew with a regular ¼" seam allowance instead of our usual scant ¼" seam allowance. Once the units were flipped open and pressed, the results were consistently sized 1½" units.

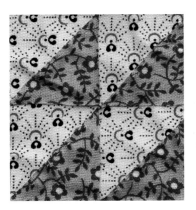

Actual size

Batch Work

Don't be daunted by all those little triangles. We found a way to presort and stitch them one row at a time. It was lovely to see those completed rows add up. Refer to "Chain Piece for Efficiency" on page 28 as needed.

1. Sort the half-square triangles into 24 sets of four matching pink pieces and four matching yellow pieces—enough for a horizontal row. Stack the sets beside your sewing machine.

2. With right sides together and long edges aligned, sew together the first pair of yellow and pink half-square triangles in the stack. Without cutting the thread, sew the second pair, the third pair, and finally the fourth matching pair. *Do not cut the thread.*

3. Continue to sew the next group of four matching pairs, and the next, and so on, until you've sewn all 96 units (24 groups of four) in the stack. Cut the chain loose after sewing the last pair, and cut the threads between each unit. Press the seam allowances toward the darker triangles and trim the "dog ears."

1½"

4. Arrange four matching units from step 3 as shown. Sew the units into pairs; press. Sew the pairs together, butting the seam allowances; press. Make 24 blocks.

Make 24.

5. Arrange the blocks from step 4 to make a horizontal row as shown. Sew the blocks together, and press the seam allowances in one direction. Label this row 1.

6. Repeat steps 1–5 to assemble the remaining 35 rows. Press the seam allowances in each row in alternate directions from row to row, and label them row 2, row 3, and so on.

Quilt Assembly and Finishing

Refer to "Finishing School" (page 84) for guidance as needed with the following steps.

1. Referring to the assembly diagram below, arrange the 36 horizontal rows as shown.

2. With right sides together, sew the rows together, carefully butting the seam allowances; press.

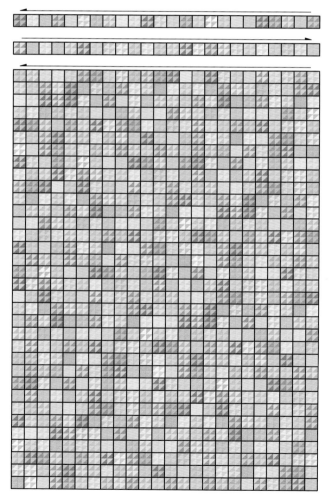

Assembly diagram

3. Layer, baste, and quilt your quilt. (Saloma quilted in the ditch diagonally across the quilt along the diagonal seams of the half-square triangles.) Use the 2¾"-wide strips to make and attach a double-fold binding, and don't forget to add a label.

LABOR OF LOVE

Relying only on memory and a single sketch from four years prior, Mary Elizabeth decided to re-create an early 1800s quilt that she had seen in antique dealer Jane Lury's "Labors of Love" booth at the first Chicago International Quilt Festival. The quilt was made from Alsatian chintz, and as you can see from Mary Elizabeth's subsequent journal notation on page 58, she explored myriad possibilities before settling on the final design.

Pieced by Mary Elizabeth Kinch, Toronto, Canada, 2007. Quilted by Lydia Bontrager.

> **Finished Size:** 88½" x 88½"
> **Finished Block:** 3" x 3"
> **Block Count:** 125

Materials

All yardages are based on 42"-wide fabric

5¾ yards *total* of red floral for stars, border, and binding

4⅞ yards of cream solid for blocks, alternate squares, and setting squares

8 yards of fabric for backing

96" x 96" piece of batting

Cutting

Cut all strips across the fabric width (selvage to selvage) unless otherwise noted.

From the *lengthwise grain* of the red floral, cut:

2 strips, 13" x 63½"

2 strips, 13" x 88½"

From the remaining red floral, cut:

500 squares, 1⅝" x 1⅝"; cut each square once diagonally to yield 1,000 half-square triangles

10 strips, 2¾" x 42"

From the cream solid, cut:

9 strips, 2¾" x 42"; crosscut into 125 squares, 2¾" x 2¾". Cut each square twice diagonally to yield 500 quarter-square triangles.

7 strips, 2" x 42"; crosscut into 125 squares, 2" x 2"

17 strips, 1¼" x 42"; crosscut into 500 squares, 1¼" x 1¼"

10 strips, 3½" x 3½"; crosscut into 100 squares, 3½" x 3½"

6 strips, 9½" x 42"; crosscut into 24 squares, 9½" x 9½"

Batch Work

With a multitude of star points, center squares, and corner squares, Mary Elizabeth recommends taking advantage of small amounts of time—10 minutes here and there—to assemble Small Star blocks. An ideal sewing session would be to assemble five Small Star blocks and, with four 3½" cream alternate blocks, create a 9½" (including seam allowance) Nine Patch Star block. Before you stop sewing, attach a 9½" cream setting block. After a few such sessions, you'll have enough stitching done to complete a crosswise row. As each row is finished, add it to the previously completed rows. By batching like this, you can have the top assembled in a surprisingly short time.

Actual size

NOTES FROM MARY ELIZABETH'S DESIGN JOURNAL

The "Labor of Love" quilt has been an interesting exercise for me. I have fond recollections of the excitement I felt when I saw the original inspiration. What I don't have is a strong memory of exactly how the quilt looked, and that is okay. That it is not going to be an exact copy, but my interpretation of it, is what makes this quilt mine. My re-creation is indicative of how many variations in quilt patterns evolved when women in years past would see a quilt somewhere and go home to re-create it, interpreting what they saw into their own creation.

The process for my quilt began with the purchase of some precious reproduction Dutch East India Company chintz fabrics from Den Haan and Wagen-makers in the Netherlands. I had small amounts and wanted to use them judiciously. I started with stars that finished at 4", which is what I have in my notes as the measurements from the original, but they looked too chunky and did not seem to represent the "feeling" I remembered from the quilt. I also felt they

looked too heavy, perhaps because of the red, so I made the next batch to finish at 3" and lightened them up by using the muslin in the center of each star. After I saw these blocks and fell in love with them, I wondered about using the chintz for the centers, so I made up a set in yellow. Again, it felt a bit heavier than I remembered. Since I also wondered about making scrappy stars, I made the final sample. In the end, 3" blocks gave me the feeling of scale I remembered from the quilt, and the muslin-centered version gave me the sentiment I remembered; that the original quilter had used up every little bit of her precious chintz to make the tiny ¾" points.

Making these samples reminded me yet again of the instinctual process that takes place when I'm designing, while at the same time it provided me a wonderful study in intensity of color. My creative play helped me sort out what I wanted this quilt to communicate: openness and thriftiness.

Samples from Mary Elizabeth's design experiments

*A Nine Patch Star block
from the finished quilt*

Assembling the Small Star Blocks

1. Sew two red half-square triangles to one cream quarter-square triangle as shown; press. Make four.

Make 4.

2. Arrange one cream 2" square, four cream 1¼" squares, and the four units from step 1 as shown. Sew the squares and units into rows; press. Sew the rows together; press.

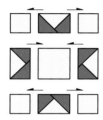

3. Repeat steps 1 and 2 to make a total of 125 small Star blocks.

Assembling the Nine Patch Star Blocks

Arrange five small Star blocks and four cream 3½" squares as shown. Sew the blocks and squares together into rows; press. Sew the rows together; press. Make 25.

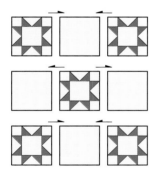 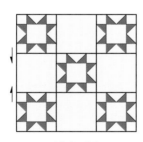

Make 25.

Quilt Assembly and Finishing

Refer to "Finishing School" (page 84) for guidance as needed with the following steps.

1. Referring to the assembly diagram above right, arrange the Nine Patch Star blocks and the 9½" cream squares in seven horizontal rows of seven blocks each, alternating them as shown.

2. Sew the blocks together into rows; press. Sew the rows together, carefully butting the seam allowances; press.

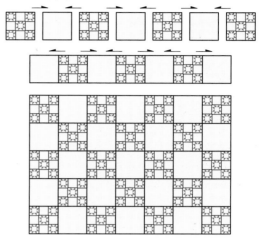

Assembly diagram

3. Sew the red 13" x 63½" borders to the sides of the quilt. Press the seam allowances toward the borders. Sew the red 13" x 88½" borders to the top and bottom; press.

4. Layer, baste, and quilt your quilt. (For the quilting in the center of the quilt, Mary Elizabeth adapted a flowered vine pattern from Gwen Marston's *Needlework Patterns*; see "Bibliography" on page 91. The pattern runs diagonally through the large open areas of the quilt, overlaying a diagonal grid. A traditional double-diagonal pattern covers the border.) Use the 2¾"-wide strips to make and attach a double-fold binding, and don't forget to add a label.

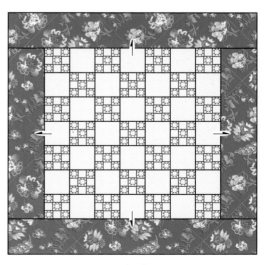

Quilt plan

Homestead Quilt

If there were ever a quilt pattern that deserved a lifetime achievement award, the Log Cabin with all its variations would certainly be a contender. It is truly a quilter's best friend. It lends itself to any size block, works beautifully with any color center square, is very forgiving if you mess up the placement of a log or accidentally stitch a piece upside down, and lends legitimacy to the claim that you need to have a few more fabrics for your Log Cabin quilt, since how can anyone prove otherwise?

So here's the challenge: Grab some fabric, play around with all the color and pattern combinations, and then try to stop after making just one! Can you think of a better excuse to drop by the local quilt shop?

The dimensions of the center squares in Biz's blocks are somewhat larger than the log widths to accomplish two things. One, the larger centers add some emphasis to the blocks. And two, the slightly expanded size helps to stabilize the first round of logs, which helps to keep the block in its proper square shape.

Finished Size: 75½" x 90½"
Finished Block: 3¾" x 3¾"
Block Count: 480

A Note about Fabrics

If you look closely at the quilt detail on page 13, you'll notice a number of key fabric choices that give this Log Cabin its vintage scrap look.

- Many darker prints from the light sides of the blocks have slipped into the dark sides of other blocks. Conversely, some of the pinks, yellows, and other medium prints appear as darks in some blocks and lights in others.

- Some of the striped fabrics have been cut with their stripes running lengthwise, some with their stripes running across the strips, and some are cut on the diagonal.

- Many logs are pieced to make use of all the short leftover strips.

- Lots of green, purple, blue, and black prints are mixed in with the key colors to prevent the quilt from looking too planned.

These are only a handful of ideas Biz borrowed from antique quilts, and they all give extra energy to the narrow little logs. Nor are these techniques restricted to Log Cabin quilts. Try them with any favorite pattern.

Materials

All yardages are based on 42"- wide fabrics.

8¼ yards *total* of assorted medium and dark prints for center squares and logs

6½ yards *total* of assorted light and medium-light prints for logs

⅔ yard of fabric for binding

5½ yards of fabric for backing

83" x 98" piece of batting

Extra rotary blades and/or rotary-blade sharpener

3 large see-through containers with lids

Actual size

Pieced by Biz Storms, Toronto, Canada, 2007.
Machine quilted by Sandra Reed. Detail on page 13.

Cutting

With so many strips to cut, Biz recommends that you begin by cutting approximately one third of both the medium and dark prints and the light and medium-light prints. As you cut, place the assorted medium and dark print strips in one large see-through container with a lid, and the light and medium-light print strips in another. Store the remaining uncut fabric in a third container for now, and replenish the other two containers by cutting additional strips as the supply of cut strips begins to run low. Cut the majority of the strips across the fabric width (selvage to selvage). See "A Note about Fabrics" on page 61 for some possible exceptions. **Note:** *Stop and sharpen or change your rotary blade after every 30 minutes of cutting. You can use this break to stretch your body as well. When you are cutting lots of fabric, it really does make a difference.*

From the assorted medium and dark prints, cut *a total of*:

480 squares, 1¼" x 1¼"

⅞"-wide strips from approximately one-third of your fabric

From the assorted light and medium-light prints, cut *a total of*:

⅞"-wide strips from approximately one third of your fabric

From the binding fabric, cut:

7 strips, 2¾" x 42"

RATHER NOT FUSS?

If you'd rather not fuss with the ⅛" markings on your ruler to cut ⅞"-wide strips, Biz suggests you cut the center squares 1½" x 1½" each, the strips 1" wide each, and then sew the blocks using a *generous* ¼" seam allowance. To do so, you will need approximately 1 yard more of both the assorted medium and dark prints and the assorted light and medium-light prints.

The blocks will finish very close to the 3¾" size noted on page 61. As long as all the blocks finish the same size, the pieces of your quilt will fit together.

Batch Work

Sewing Log Cabin blocks in batches makes perfect sense, especially since you will be using different lengths of ⅞"-wide strips. Follow the first four steps of the instructions below, and you will have a supply of center squares with "logs" (strips) on all four sides.

From that point, you can switch to working on only 15 or 20 blocks to add the second round. For the third round, add another 15 to 20 units so you will be sewing on 30 to 40 blocks, but in two different sizes. Continue adding extra units each time you start with the light strips, so as you progress with the blocks, you will be working on blocks in four different sizes.

Here's the payoff: Once you get to this stage, every time you complete a round you will have 15 to 20 finished blocks! Just keep adding 15 to 20 one-round units and then more center squares every time you start a new round with light strips. As the strips grow shorter, you can use the shorter lengths on the smaller units. Refer to "Chain Piece for Efficiency" on page 28 as needed.

1. Begin with 100 center squares and 10 different light strips. With right sides together, chain piece ten 1¼" center squares to each strip. Cut the chain loose after sewing the last square in each strip, and cut the units apart. (If the units are closely spaced, you do not need to trim the little bits of fabric in between.) Carefully press the seam allowances away from the center squares.

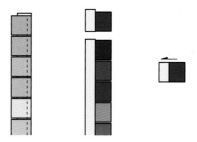

2. Shuffle the units from step 1 and place them right side down in a stack beside your sewing machine with the light strip facing you in the six o'clock position. Pull 10 new strips from the container of assorted lights and chain piece the units from step 1, right sides together, to these new light strips.

Cut the chain loose after sewing the last unit in each strip, and cut the units apart. Carefully press the seam allowances away from the center squares.

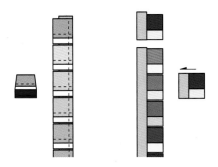

3. Shuffle the units from step 2 and place them right side down in a stack beside your sewing machine with the second light strip facing you in the six o'clock position. Pull 10 strips from the container of assorted darks and chain piece the units from step 2, right sides together, to these dark strips. Cut the chain loose after sewing the last unit in each strip, and cut the units apart. Carefully press the seam allowances away from the center squares.

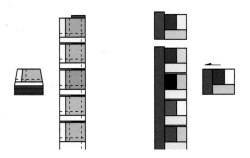

4. Shuffle the units from step 3 and place them right side down in a stack beside your sewing machine with the dark strip facing you in the six o'clock position. Pull 10 new strips from the container of assorted darks and chain piece the units from step 3, right sides together, to these strips. Cut the chain loose after sewing the last unit in each strip, and cut the units apart. Carefully press the seam allowances away from the center squares and trim any overhang on the last dark strip.

Trim.

5. Shuffle the units from step 4 and place them right side down in a stack beside your sewing machine with the second dark strip facing you in the six o'clock position. Repeat steps 1–4 to add three additional rounds of light and dark strips to the blocks.

6. Repeat steps 1–5 to make a total of 480 blocks.

Quilt Assembly and Finishing

Refer to "Finishing School" (page 84) for guidance as needed with the following steps.

1. Press the blocks thoroughly and, referring to the assembly diagram below, arrange them in 24 horizontal rows of 20 blocks each. Biz chose a zigzag pattern known as "Streak of Lightning," but you can choose any setting you like.

2. Sew the blocks together; press. Sew the rows together, carefully butting the seam allowances; press.

Assembly diagram

3. Layer, baste, and quilt your quilt. (The quilt on page 62 is quilted in an overall feather motif.) Use the 2¾"-wide strips to make and attach a double-fold binding, and don't forget to add a label.

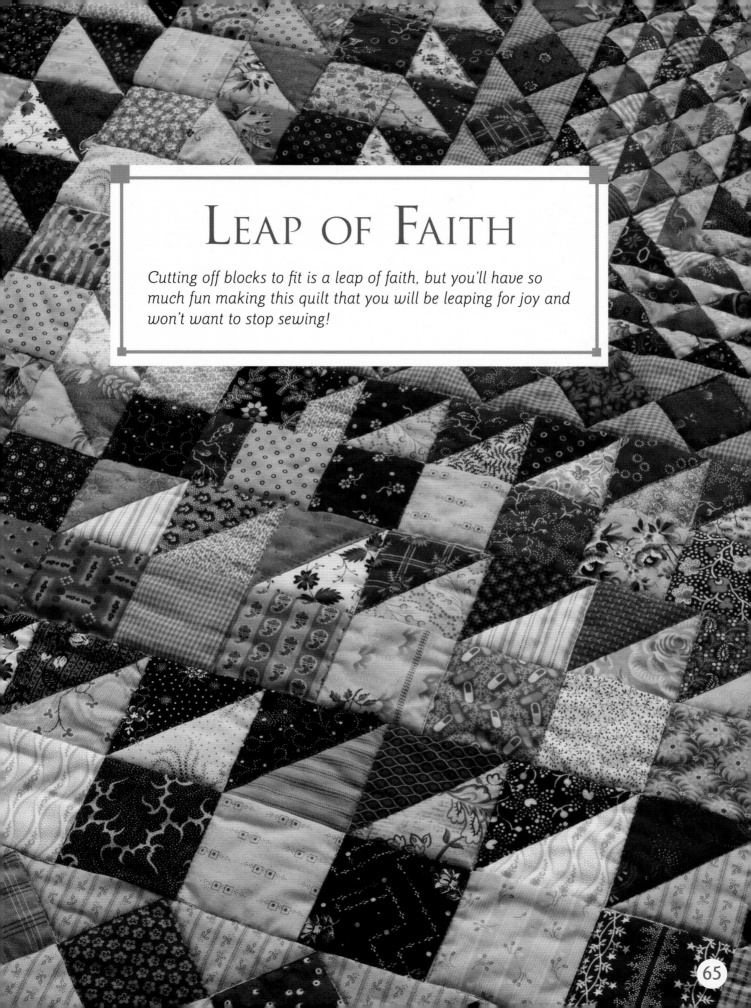

LEAP OF FAITH

Cutting off blocks to fit is a leap of faith, but you'll have so much fun making this quilt that you will be leaping for joy and won't want to stop sewing!

Pieced by Mary Elizabeth Kinch, Toronto, Canada, 2007.
Machine quilted by Sandra Reed. Detail on page 26.

Finished Size: 78¾" x 78¾"

Materials

All yardages are based on 42"- wide fabric.

6½ yards *total* of medium-light fabrics for blocks, units, triangles, and squares

5¾ yards *total* of medium-dark to dark fabrics for blocks, units, triangles, and squares

⅞ yards of fabric for binding

7¼ yards of fabric for backing

87" x 87" piece of batting

Cutting

Cut all strips across the fabric width (selvage to selvage).

From the assorted medium-light fabrics, cut *a total of*:

2 squares, 2" x 2"; cut each square once diagonally to yield 4 half-square triangles

679 squares 1⅞" x 1⅞"; cut each square once diagonally to yield 1,358 half-square triangles

22 squares, 3⅜" x 3⅜"; cut each square twice diagonally to yield 88 quarter-square triangles

28 squares, 2⅝" x 2⅝"; cut each square once diagonally to yield 56 half square triangles

224 squares, 2¼" x 2¼"; cut 192 squares once diagonally to yield 384 half-square triangles

36 squares, 2½" x 2½"

34 squares, 3⅛" x 3⅛", cut each square once diagonally to yield 68 half-square triangles

38 squares, 2¾" x 2¾"

32 squares, 2⅞" x 2⅞", cut each square once diagonally to yield 64 half-square triangles

87 squares 4⅛" x 4⅛" cut each square twice diagonally to yield 348 quarter-square triangles

40 squares, 4¼" x 4¼"; crosscut each square twice diagonally to yield 160 quarter-square triangles

From the assorted medium-dark to dark fabrics, cut *a total of*:

1 square, 1¹⁵⁄₁₆" x 1¹⁵⁄₁₆" *

143 squares, 3¼" x 3¼"; crosscut each square twice diagonally to yield 572 quarter-square triangles. You will have three triangles left over.

110 squares, 1⅞" x 1⅞", cut each square once diagonally to yield 220 half-square triangles

2 squares, 2⅜" x 2⅜"; cut each square once diagonally to yield 4 half-square triangles

57 squares, 2¾" x 2¾"; cut 11 squares twice diagonally to yield 44 quarter-square triangles

40 squares, 2" x 2"

28 squares, 2⅝" x 2⅝"; cut each square once diagonally to yield 56 half-square triangles

232 squares, 2¼" x 2¼"; cut 192 squares once diagonally to yield 384 half-square triangles

216 squares, 2½" x 2½"

32 squares, 2⅞" x 2⅞"; cut each square once diagonally to yield 64 half-square triangles

34 squares, 3⅛" x 3⅛", cut each square once diagonally to yield 68 half-square triangles

40 squares, 4¼" x 4¼"; crosscut each square twice diagonally to yield 160 quarter-square triangles

*Use a ruler with a ⅛" grid and eyeball the center of the two grid lines to achieve the necessary measurement.

From the binding fabric, cut:

9 strips, 2¾" x 42"

Batch Work

By setting up the pieces for different border rounds, and working on them when you have a few minutes here and there, the quilt grows quickly and easily.

Notes from Mary Elizabeth's Design Journal

The inspiration for this quilt came from many places. It is one time when Lord Alfred Tennyson's quote really stands true with regards to quiltmaking: "We are a part of all whom we have met." The center of the quilt was inspired by an 1880s crib quilt. I loved the square-on-point borders I had seen in the Australian "Rajah Quilt" (page 24). I knew I needed some flying-geese rounds (I am just prepping myself for making the Shelburne's "Flying Geese Medallion" on page 20!), and an antique quilt top in Biz's collection provided the idea of graduated borders, alternating half-square-triangle units with scrappy squares.

The "big leap" here was to apply a design concept that quiltmaker Gwen Marston has been talking about and teaching for years. In her study of old quilts, she has seen many instances where a quiltmaker simply cut something off if it did not fit, or added something on if it needed to be bigger. Easier said than done for me—chop up a block? Heresy!

Once I decided to take the plunge, what fun I had! I knew I wanted to work in rich colors that were lower in contrast, but not totally blended. I also wanted to shake up the mix of greenish golds and taupes with browns, blacks, and splashes of blue, which I knew from studying old quilts would give my quilt life.

The center medallion required some intense scrutiny to achieve the outward movement of the original, and I saw quickly that I would need to choose a focus color for each of the outward rounds. To create a visual break, I strove for a definitive band of pieced borders in the outer third of the quilt. By mixing darks and darker mediums with splashes of brighter golds, I got exactly the effect I was hoping for. I really enjoyed playing with color and had a blast seeing the combinations that occurred with the random pairings of fabrics in each block.

Assembling the Center Medallion

For purposes of simplicity, the assorted medium-light fabrics will be referred to as "light" and the assorted medium-dark/dark fabrics will be referred to as "dark" in the remaining instructions for this quilt.

1. With right sides together and matching center points, sew light 2" half-square triangles to opposite sides of the dark $1^{15}/_{16}$" square as shown; press. Repeat to sew light 2" half-square triangles to the remaining sides; press. Trim the unit to measure $2^{1}/_{2}$" x $2^{1}/_{2}$".

2. Sew a light $1^{7}/_{8}$" half-square triangle to one short edge of a dark $3^{1}/_{4}$" quarter-square triangle as shown; press. Sew a matching light half-square triangle to the remaining short edge; press. Make 569 flying-geese units.

Make 569.

3. Sew 11 flying-geese units from step 2 together to make a row as shown; press. Make four rows. Set the remaining flying-geese units aside for now.

Make 4.

4. Sew a dark $1^{7}/_{8}$" half-square triangle and a light $1^{7}/_{8}$" half-square triangle together along their long edges to make a half-square-triangle unit; press. Make 220 half-square-triangle units.

Make 220.

5. Arrange 55 units from step 4 and 11 dark 2¾" quarter-square triangles as shown. Sew the units and triangles together into rows; press. Sew the rows together; press. Make four.

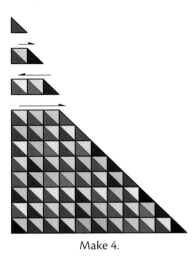

Make 4.

6. Arrange and sew the center square from step 1, the four flying-geese rows from step 3, the four units from step 5, and the four dark 2⅜" half-square triangles as shown; press.

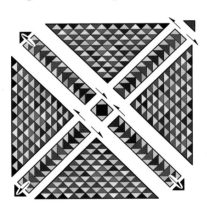

Assembling and Adding the Borders

Your quilt might look slightly different than the quilt shown on page 66 due to the "leap of faith" method used for trimming the various borders. The numbers shown in "Cutting" on page 67 and in the following instructions are based on the true mathematical measurements of the growing quilt as each border is added. If however, you find you are short a piece or two as the result of how you've trimmed things up, there is sufficient fabric allowed for you to cut and add a few extra pieces or units if you need them.

1. **For border 1,** sew light 3⅜" quarter-square triangles to opposite sides of a dark 2" square as shown; press. Make 40. Sew nine units together as shown; press. Make two. Sew 11 units together; press. Make two.

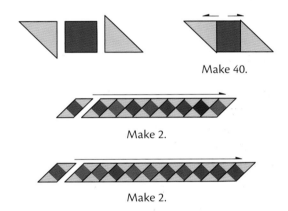

Make 40.

Make 2.

Make 2.

2. Sew a remaining light 3⅜" quarter-square triangle to opposite ends of each strip from step 1 as shown; press. Trim the ends of each strip, leaving a ¼" seam allowance. Referring to the assembly diagram on page 70, sew the nine-unit borders to the sides of the center medallion, and the 11-unit borders to the top and bottom. Press the seam allowances away from the center medallion.

¼"

Assembly diagram

3. **For border 2,** sew a dark 2⅝" half-square triangle and a light 2⅝" half-square triangle together along their long edges to make a half-square-triangle unit as shown; press. Make 56. Sew the units together to make a single long border strip.

Make 56.

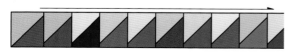

Sew together to make one long strip.

4. Measure the quilt through the center from top to bottom, and from side to side. (These measurements should be the same.) Cut four strips to this measurement from the long border strip you made in step 3. (You may be cutting right through the center of a half-square-triangle unit. Remember: the quilt is called "Leap of Faith.")

5. Referring to the assembly diagram, sew two strips from step 4 to the sides of the quilt. Press the seam allowances toward the strips. Sew a dark 2¼" square to each end of the remaining strips. Press the seam allowances toward the strips and sew them to the top and bottom of the quilt; press.

6. **For border 3,** sew 32 light 2¼" squares and 32 dark 2¼" squares together, alternating the values to make a single long border strip. Press the seam allowances in one direction.

7. Measure the quilt through the center from top to bottom, and from side to side. (These measurements should be the same.) Cut four strips to this measurement.

8. Repeat step 5 using the strips you cut in step 7, and using four dark 2¼" squares for cornerstones.

9. **For border 4,** sew a dark 2⅞" half-square triangle and a light 2⅞" half-square triangle together along their long edges to make a half-square-triangle unit; press. Make 64. Sew the units together as shown in the diagram following step 3 to make a single long border strip.

10. Measure the quilt through the center from top to bottom, and from side to side. (These measurements should be the same.) Cut four strips to this measurement, and repeat step 5 to sew these strips to the quilt using four dark 2½" squares for cornerstones.

11. **For border 5,** sew 36 light 2½" squares and 36 dark 2½" squares together, alternating the values to make a single long border strip. Press the seam allowances in one direction. Measure the quilt through the center from top to bottom, and from side to side. (These measurements should be the same.) Cut four strips to this measurement.

12. Repeat step 5 using the strips you cut in step 11, and using four dark 2½" squares for cornerstones.

13. **For border 6,** sew a dark 3⅛" half-square triangle and a light 3⅛" half-square triangle together along their long edges to make a half-square-triangle unit; press. Make 68. Sew the units together as shown in the diagram following step 3 to make a single long border strip.

14. Measure the quilt through the center from top to bottom, and from side to side. (These measurements should be the same.) Cut four strips to this measurement, and repeat step 5 to sew these strips to the quilt using four dark 2¾" squares for cornerstones.

15. **For border 7,** sew 38 light 2¾" squares and 38 dark 2¾" squares together, alternating the values to make a single long border strip. Press the seam allowances in one direction. Measure the quilt through the center from top to bottom, and from side to side. (These measurements should be the same.) Cut four strips to this measurement.

16. Repeat step 5 using the strips you cut in step 15, and using four dark 2¾" squares for cornerstones.

17. **For border 8,** sew light 4⅛" quarter-square triangles to opposite sides of a dark 2½" square as shown; press. Make 72 and sew them together to make a single long border strip. Sew a remaining light 4⅛" quarter-square triangle to opposite ends of the row as shown; press. Trim the ends of the strip, leaving a ¼" seam allowance.

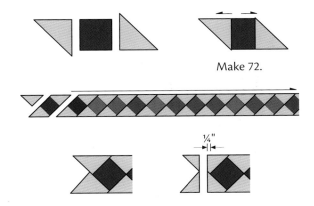

Make 72.

18. Measure the quilt through the center from top to bottom. Cut two strips to this measurement and, referring to the assembly diagram, sew them to the sides of the quilt. Press the seam allowances away from the newly added border. Measure the quilt through the center from side to side, including the borders just added. Cut two strips to this measurement and sew them to the top and bottom; press.

19. **For border 9,** sew together as shown 220 flying-geese units that were set aside in "Assembling the Center Medallion," step 2; press. Repeat step 18 to measure, cut, and sew flying-geese borders to the sides, top, and bottom of the quilt; press.

Sew together 220 flying-geese units.

20. **For border 10,** sew a dark 4¼" quarter-square triangle and a light 4¼" quarter-square triangle together along one short side as shown. Make 160. With right sides together, long edges aligned, and opposing seam allowances carefully butted, sew two triangle units together; press. Make 80.

Make 80.

21. Referring to the assembly diagram, sew the units from step 20 together to make a single long border strip; press. Repeat step 18 to measure, cut, and sew borders to the sides, top, and bottom of the quilt; press.

22. **For borders 11 and 12,** sew a dark 2¼" half-square triangle and a light 2¼" half-square triangle together along their long edges to make a half-square-triangle unit; press. Make 384. Sew 192 units together to make a long border strip as shown; press. Make two.

Make 384.

Make 2 long strips.

23. Sew the two strips from step 22 together as shown; press. Measure the quilt through the center from side to side. Cut two strips to this measurement and, referring to the assembly diagram, sew them to the top and bottom of the quilt. Press the seam allowances away from the newly added border. Measure the quilt through the center from top to bottom, including the borders just added. Cut two strips to this measurement and sew them to the sides; press.

24. **For border 13,** repeat step 17 to make a single long border using 100 dark 2½" squares and 202 light 4⅛" quarter-square triangles. Repeat step 18 to measure, cut, and sew borders to the sides, top, and bottom of the quilt; press.

25. **For border 14,** sew the remaining 305 flying-geese units together; press. Repeat step 22 to measure, cut, and sew flying-geese borders to the top, bottom, and sides of the quilt; press.

Finishing

Proceed to "Finishing School" on page 84 for guidance in layering, basting, quilting, and otherwise finishing your quilt. (The quilt on page 66 was quilted in the ditch around every triangle and square.) Use the 2¾"-wide strips to make and attach a double-fold binding, and don't forget to add a label.

GUEST ROOM QUILT

Old Swedish Quilts *and* Quilts in the Dutch Tradition *(see "Bibliography" on page 91)* are two books that have influenced both of us in our quiltmaking. Common to these books is a distinctive style of antique quilt not often seen in our North American examples. These quilts begin with a small center block (or area) that contains either elaborate appliqué or intricate piecing. The centerpiece is then surrounded with hundreds of larger, simple pieced blocks that unify the overall design. Many of these quilts also incorporate wide chintz or other large-scale print borders as a frame.

Biz decided to add her own spin to this quiltmaking style by showing Broken Dishes blocks in two different sizes, with a subtle color variation in the center area. (Note the one rust block in the midst of the blue blocks in the center of the quilt on page 74. It adds a bit of feistiness while still allowing the smaller blocks to provide a calm, restful place in the midst of all the larger blocks, with their higher energy level.)

Mary Elizabeth and Biz both adore this quilt, and although Biz is the proud owner, Mary Elizabeth has declared that it will go in the guest room whenever she comes to visit.

Pieced by Biz Storms, Toronto, Canada, 2007.
Hand quilted by Emma Hostetler. Detail on page 12.

Finished Size: 72½" x 72½"
Finished Blocks: 4" x 4" (large block);
2" x 2" (small block)
Large Block Count: 308
Small Block Count: 64

Materials

All yardages are based on 42"- wide fabric.

4 yards *total* of assorted light prints for large and small blocks

3⅝ yards *total* of assorted medium and dark prints for large blocks

⅜ yard *total* of assorted medium and dark blue prints for small blocks

Scrap of dark rust print for small blocks

⅔ yard of fabric for binding

4½ yards of fabric for backing

80" x 80" batting

Cutting

Cut all strips across the fabric width (selvage to selvage).

From the assorted light prints, cut *a total of*:

32 squares, 3¼" x 3¼"; cut each square twice diagonally to yield 128 quarter-square triangles

154 squares, 5¼" x 5¼"; cut each square twice diagonally to yield 616 quarter-square triangles

From the assorted medium and dark blue prints, cut *a total of*:

32 squares, 3¼" x 3¼"; cut each square twice diagonally to yield 128 quarter-square triangles. You will have two triangles left over.

From the scrap of dark rust print, cut:

1 square, 3¼" x 3¼"; cut twice diagonally to yield 4 quarter-square triangles. You will have two triangles left over.

From the assorted medium and dark prints, cut *a total of*:

154 squares, 5¼" x 5¼"; cut each square twice diagonally to yield 616 quarter-square triangles

From the binding fabric, cut:

8 strips, 2¾" x 42"

Actual size

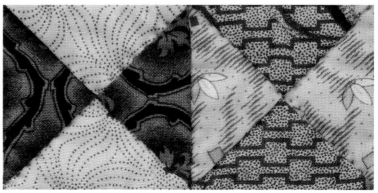

Batch Work

This quilt divides naturally into five sections for batch work. Chain piecing makes the piecing proceed easily and efficiently; refer to "Chain Piece for Efficiency" on page 28 as needed. Once the blocks are made, you can work on assembly one section at a time. Check the direction of the seams in the adjacent blocks before pressing the rows in the adjoining sections.

1. Sort the small quarter-square triangles into matching pairs.

2. Place the triangles you paired in step 1 in two stacks: small light triangles and small medium or dark blue and rust triangles. Work randomly so that identical pairs are not grouped together in either stack.

3. With right sides together, sew the top triangles from each stack together along one short side as shown. Without cutting the thread, sew the next light and medium or dark triangles together. (These should match the first two triangles). Continue chain piecing until you have reached the end of both stacks; cut the chain loose after sewing the last pair. You should have 128 triangle units in matching pairs.

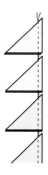

4. Cut the threads between each unit; press the seam allowances toward the darker triangles and carefully sort the units into two identical stacks as you go. Each stack should contain one of the matching triangle pairs.

5. With right sides together, long edges aligned, and opposing seam allowances carefully butted, sew the top unit from each stack together. Continue chain piecing until you have reached the end of both stacks. Cut the chain loose after sewing the last pair. Cut the threads between each unit and press. You now have 64 small blocks.

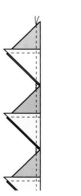

Make 64.

6. Referring to section 1 of the assembly diagram on page 77, arrange the small blocks in eight rows of eight blocks each, rotating the blocks as shown, and placing the light/rust block near the center. Sew the blocks into rows. Press the seam allowances in alternating directions from row to row. Sew the rows together, carefully butting the seam allowances; press. Label this section 1.

7. Repeat steps 1–5 using the large light quarter-square triangles and the large medium and dark quarter-square triangles. Make 308 large blocks.

Make 308.

8. Referring to sections 2 and 3 of the assembly diagram, arrange 28 large blocks in four horizontal rows of seven blocks each, rotating the blocks as shown. Sew the blocks into rows. Press the seam allowances in alternating directions from row to row. Sew the rows together; press. Make two total and label them section 2 and section 3.

9. Referring to sections 4 and 5 of the assembly diagram, arrange 126 large blocks in seven horizontal rows of 18 blocks each, rotating the blocks as shown. Sew the blocks into rows. Press the seam allowances in alternating directions from row to row. Sew the rows together; press. Make two total and label them section 4 and section 5.

Quilt Assembly and Finishing

Refer to "Finishing School" (page 84) for guidance as needed with the following steps.

1. Referring to the assembly diagram below, arrange the five sections of the quilt as shown. Sew sections 1, 2, and 3 together; press. Sew section 4 to the top and section 5 to the bottom; press.

2. Layer, baste, and quilt your quilt. (The quilt on page 74 is quilted in the ditch around each triangle.) Use the 2¾"-wide strips to make and attach a double-fold binding, and don't forget to add a label.

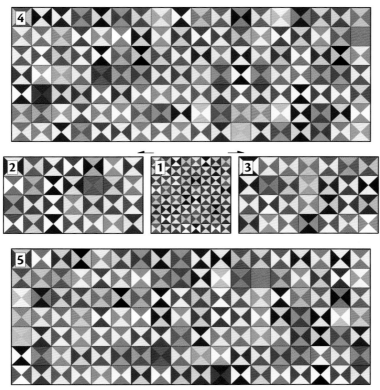

Assembly diagram

NORTHERN LIGHTS

Diminutive stars sparkle and dance, bursting gaily across this quilt. Mary Elizabeth has never seen for herself, but has heard how the Northern Lights also dance across the sky, often displaying a wonderful shade of green, which inspired the color for this quilt.

Mary Elizabeth chose a different green print for the points of each star, and then paired these with a variety of brown prints—and a couple of unexpected purples—for the star centers. As she was designing the quilt, trying to decide on the size and placement for the circular star units, she made just one unit and used it to make multiple color photocopies. By placing the copies on her design wall, she was able to experiment with spacing between the stars and to imagine what type of quilting might fill in the vast areas of background. By the time she approached Sandra Reed to do the quilting, Mary Elizabeth knew that she wanted a traditional, undulating, double-spined, feathered vine. Sandra's idea to "basket weave" the vine adds substantially to the overall design and makes us smile when we look at the finished quilt.

Finished Size: 58" x 81"
Finished Star Unit: 5" diameter
Finished Overall Block: 11½" x 11½"
Block Count: 35

Materials

All yardages are based on 42"- wide fabric.

7 yards of cream solid for star backgrounds, setting blocks, and binding

1⅔ yards *total* of assorted medium-dark green prints for star points

⅓ yard *total* of assorted brown and purple prints for star centers

5⅛ yards of fabric for backing

66" x 89" piece of batting

Large sheet of see-through template material*

*For example, 12" x 12" or 11" x 14"

Cutting

Use the patterns on page 83 to make templates for the star points (A), star background (B), and star center (C) from see-through template material. Make small holes in the templates for matching seam intersections as indicated by the small dot on the pattern pieces, and transfer the dots to the fabric pieces as you cut them. Cut all strips across the fabric width (selvage to selvage).

From the assorted medium-dark green prints, cut *a total of* :

420 A pieces in matching sets of 12

From the cream solid, cut:

12 strips, 12" x 42"; crosscut into 35 squares, 12" x 12"

8 strips, 2¾" x 42"

420 B pieces

From the assorted brown and purple prints, cut *a total of*:

35 C pieces

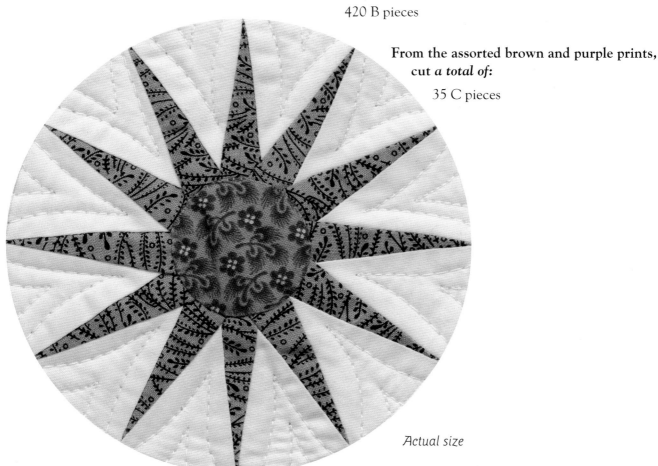

Actual size

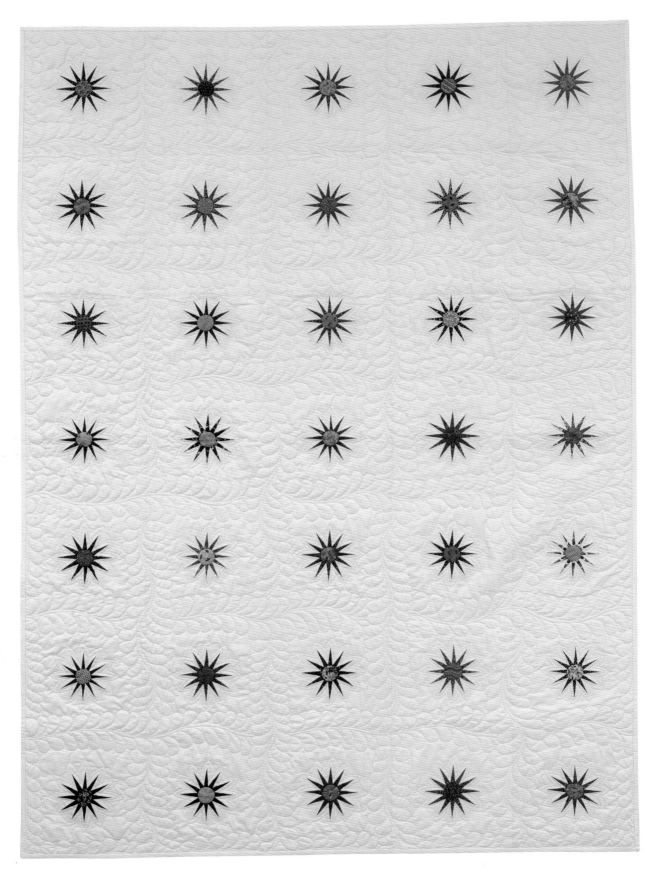

Pieced by Mary Elizabeth Kinch, Toronto, Canada, 2007.
Machine quilted by Sandra Reed. Detail on page 82.

Batch Work

The instructions below walk you through the process of making a single large Star block (including setting the star unit into the background). However, if you prefer, you can assemble the individual star units first, in a single sitting, one at a time, or in batches, depending on the time you have available. Then you can set them in the background squares in another batch-work session.

The star units assemble equally well by hand or by machine. They make handy little pocket projects for stitching a few seams when you have a moment free.

Assembling the Star Units

1. Lay out 12 matching green A pieces and 12 cream B pieces as shown to make a star. With right sides together, sew one A piece to an adjacent B piece using the dots to match the key points. Finger-press the seam allowances toward B.

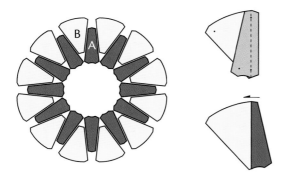

2. Sew the adjacent B piece to the opposite side of A as shown; finger-press. Continue around the circle, adding A and B pieces in order until the circle is complete. This continuous method, rather than sewing in sections, ensures a nice, flat, fan effect in the seams.

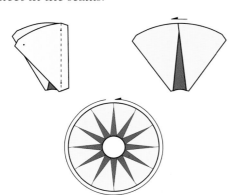

Assembling the Large Star Blocks

1. Use template material and the pattern on page 83 to make a template for preparing the background square. Fold a 12" cream square in half vertically and horizontally and press lightly to form creased guidelines. Open the first fold (the square is now folded in half), place the template so the edge is on the fold line as shown, and lightly trace the half circle onto the fabric. Remove the template and cut directly on the curved line. Unfold the square.

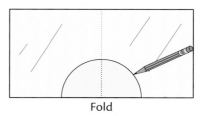
Fold

2. With right sides together, set a star unit into the hole in the background square, carefully matching and pinning the points at twelve, three, six, and nine o'clock with the crease lines you made in step 1. Ease in the rest of the star circle, matching raw edges and pinning copiously. Stitch the circle into the background and press the seam allowances toward the background block.

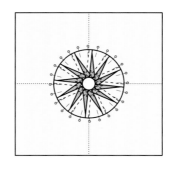

APPLIQUÉ ALTERNATIVE

For those who enjoy appliqué, our friend Nancy Ray suggests using reverse appliqué to place the star circle in the background square.

3. Use your preferred method to appliqué a center circle (piece C) to the center of the star.

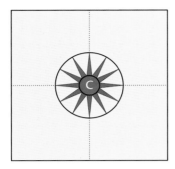

4. Repeat steps 1–3 to make a total of 35 large Star blocks.

Quilt Assembly and Finishing

Refer to "Finishing School" (page 84) for guidance as needed with the following steps.

1. Referring to the assembly diagram below, arrange the blocks in seven horizontal rows of five blocks each.

2. Sew the blocks together; press. Sew the rows together, carefully butting the seam allowances; press.

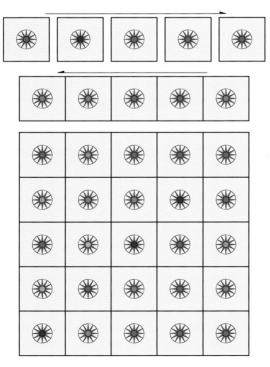

Assembly diagram

3. Layer, baste, and quilt your quilt. (In the quilt shown on page 80, the small, individual stars are outlined with a simple flower motif. The open areas between the stars are quilted with lush feathered vine worked in a basket-weave fashion.) Use the 2¾"-wide strips to make and attach a double-fold binding, and don't forget to add a label.

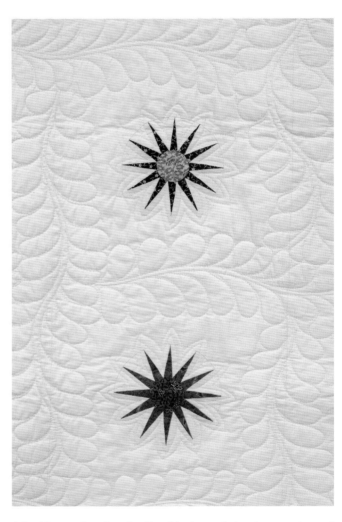

Machine quilter Sandra Reed balanced the sharp points of each star by outlining them in a gentle curved-petal motif.

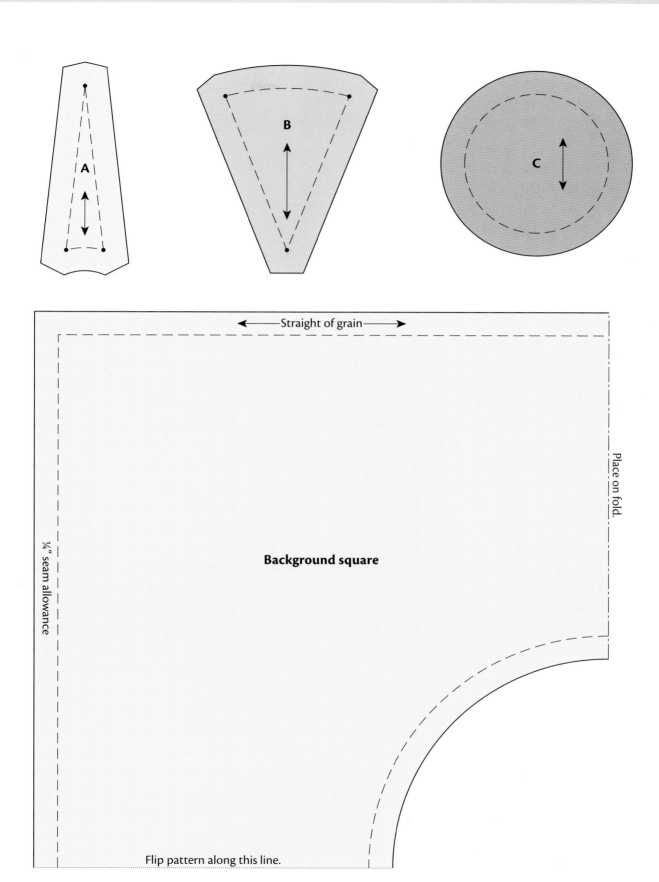

A

B

C

Straight of grain

Place on fold.

¼" seam allowance

Background square

Flip pattern along this line.

If you have an armful of blocks ready to assemble into a quilt top, you are in the right place!

Assembling a Quilt Top

We like to assemble our quilt tops using a random approach, by which we mean we simply stitch the top together without prearranging the block placement. The result is an unpredictable placement of color that adds charm and originality to the quilt and is almost impossible to plan. It's another leap of faith, but give it a try. Make sure you know the number of rows of blocks you need and how many blocks are in each row before you start, and then place the blocks into a container so you can pick them without looking.

1. Referring to "Chain Piece for Efficiency" on page 28, chain piece the first two rows of blocks together. (If you are making the "Homestead Quilt" on page 60, be careful to maintain the log-cabin setting you've chosen.) Cut the thread loose when you get to the ends of the row, but *do not cut the threads between the blocks*.

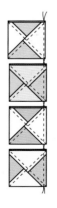
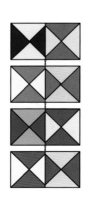

2. Working one row at a time, continue chain piecing the remaining rows to the chain from step 1. Once again, cut the thread loose when you get to the bottom of each row, but *do not cut the threads between the blocks*. When you've finished sewing all the blocks into rows, press the seam allowances in alternating directions from row to row.

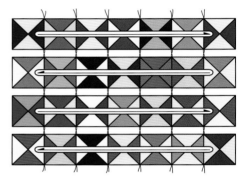

3. Stitch the rows together, carefully butting the seam allowances for perfect intersections. Press the seam allowances in one direction.

Setting Blocks On Point

Assembling a quilt top with its blocks on point can result in an attractive, vibrant set, but the process can be rather fiddly and time consuming. For this reason—sadly—many quilters choose to avoid the on-point set.

Let us allay those fears! We have developed a somewhat unorthodox method to stitch an on-point set by converting it back to a more familiar horizontal/vertical orientation. We call our method "economy block assembly" since its construction resembles the traditional Economy block. Assembly is broken into five distinct stages, so you can realize significant progress quickly.

1. Tilt a sheet of ¼" graph paper on point. Draft your quilt top onto the tilted graph paper using one square for each block, half squares for the side setting triangles, and quarter squares for the corner setting triangles.

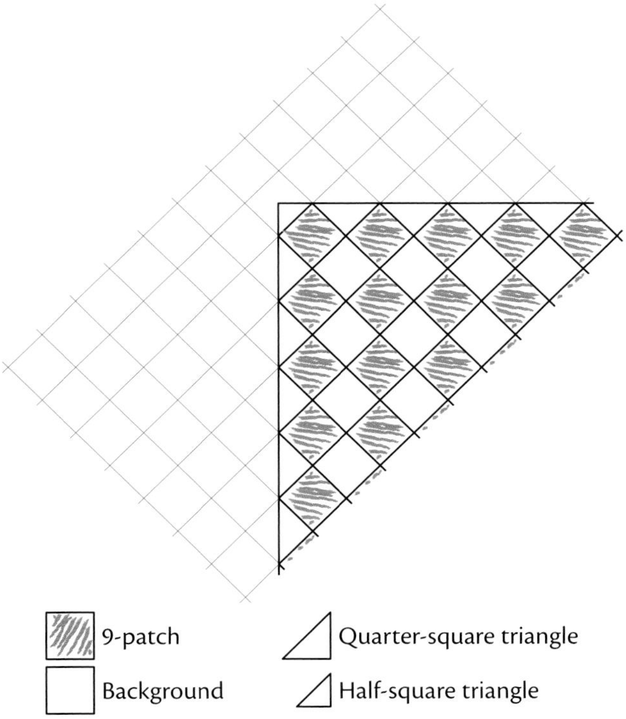

2. Return the graph paper to its normal orientation and, in pencil, outline the largest possible square in the center of your quilt. (Expect an irregularly shaped fourth side when your quilt is rectangular.) Write the number of blocks (and/or triangles) for the sides of the square and for the long sides of each of the four corner pieces.

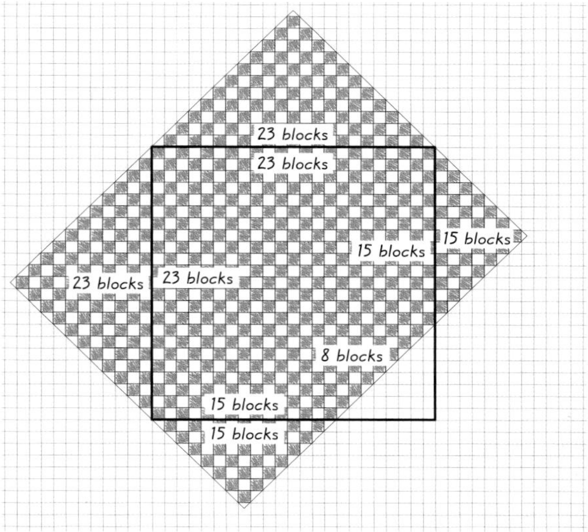

3. Stitch the blocks that form the center square together as described in "Assembling a Quilt Top" steps 1–3.

4. Stitch one corner unit together, starting with the longest row and incorporating blocks and *quarter-square* side setting triangles as shown. Use a *half-square* corner setting triangle at the peak of the section; this forms a corner of the quilt.

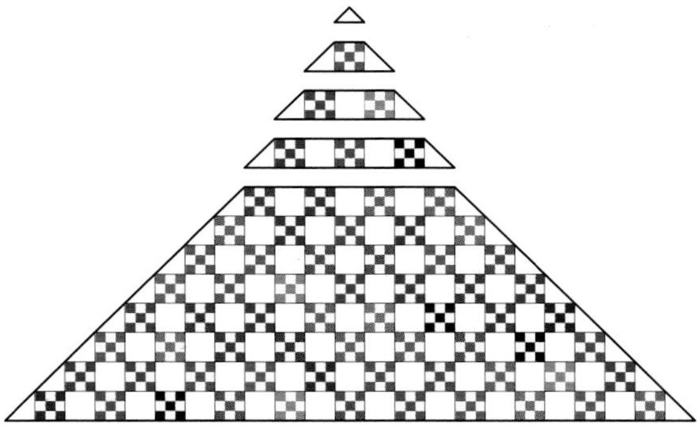

5. Press the seam allowances of the corner section in the opposite direction to the direction you pressed the seam allowances in the center square. Stitch the corner unit onto the appropriate side of the center square, carefully butting the seam allowances; press.

6. Repeat steps 4 and 5 to complete the remaining three corner sections and sew them to the quilt center; press.

Marking Quilting Designs

We have a very simple approach when it comes to quilting these small-block quilts. We prefer simple allover designs such as grids, or clamshells, or in-the-ditch stitching that follows the seam lines around the individual shapes and/or blocks. Neither approach requires that the quilt top be marked prior to layering and basting.

For quilts with lots of open space suitable for more elaborate quilting, such as "Labor of Love" (page 56) or "Northern Lights" (page 80), you may want to mark before layering and basting while the quilt top is lighter and easier to handle. There are numerous marking pencils and other marking products available at quilt shops and on the internet. Our preference is to use a pencil with a fairly hard lead, a soapstone marker, a Hera marker, or a chalk liner for marking. These options work well for both hand and machine quilting.

Experiment to see which products you like best, and which are most suitable for and easiest to remove from the fabrics you are using. We also recommend that you speak with other quilters; they are often your best source of information.

Layering

You've put lots of love and effort into piecing your beautiful quilt top, so be sure to invest in batting and backing materials that are worthy of your work and will stand the test of time. To re-create an antique appearance (and to offset the weight and bulk of so many seam allowances!), we both prefer thin, flat battings made from natural fibers. For the quilts in this book, we've used some of our favorites, including Quilters Dream Select, Hobbs Cotton Organic, Hobbs Tuscany Silk, and Hobbs Tuscany 100% Cotton.

The following instructions work for quilters who hand quilt and for machine quilting on a domestic sewing machine.

1. Carefully press the quilt top and lay it out on a clean, flat surface. Measure and mark the center of each side with a pin. Loosely roll the top and bottom ends of the quilt toward the center, stopping just before the center pins, and carefully move the rolled quilt aside.

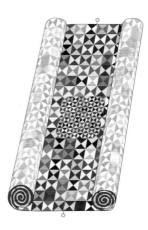

2. Prepare a backing for your quilt that extends approximately 4" beyond your quilt top on all sides. To piece the backing, divide the backing fabric crosswise (selvage to selvage) into two or three panels of equal length, depending upon the size of the quilt. Remove the selvages and sew the panels together along the lengthwise edges with a ¼" seam allowance. Press the seam allowance(s) open and iron the backing to remove any wrinkles.

3. Place the backing right side down on a clean, flat surface. Tape one long edge to the surface and mark the center of the taped edge with a pin. Gently position the rest of the backing so that it is flat and wrinkle free, and tape it to the surface. Once again, mark the center of the taped edge with a pin. Repeat to tape and pin the remaining two edges.

4. Center the batting on top of the backing, shifting gently to remove any wrinkles. Cut away any excess batting so it lies just inside the outer edges of the backing, and so the pins you placed in step 3 are visible.

5. Pick up the rolled quilt top from each side so it folds in half, and position it across the center of the batting, matching the side center pins on the quilt top with those on the backing. There should be equal amounts of batting and backing visible on each side.

6. Carefully unroll each end of the quilt top so the center pins for the quilt top and backing line up at the top and bottom, and even amounts of batting and backing are visible on the top and bottom edges. If the top becomes a little skewed, roll the ends back to the center and start again.

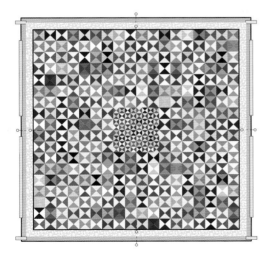

Basting for Hand Quilting

1. Baste around the perimeter of the layered quilt top about ¼" inside the edge using white thread and a long running stitch. This stabilizes the layers and helps keep the edges straight for binding.

2. Beginning on one side, baste about 6" inside the perimeter row of stitching using the same running stitch and white thread. Continue to work your way across the quilt, basting a line of stitches every 6" until you reach the center. Remove the tape and gently roll the layered sandwich so you can continue basting in the same manner until you reach the other side of the quilt and the entire sandwich is basted in one direction.

3. Unroll the sandwich, re-tape, and repeat step 2 to baste the quilt in the opposite direction to complete a 6" grid. You are now ready to proceed to "Quilting" on page 88.

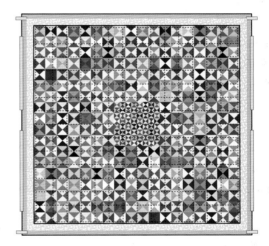

Basting for Machine Quilting

1. You will need a large supply of small, rustproof safety pins. Insert a pin every 3" around the perimeter of the layered quilt top about ¼" inside the edge. This stabilizes the layers and helps keep the edges straight for binding. Try not to shift the layers, and leave the pins open for now.

2. Beginning on one side, insert a row of pins about 4" in from the edge of the quilt top, spacing the pins roughly 4" apart. Continue to work your way across the quilt, inserting a line of pins every 4" until you reach the center. (Try to avoid pinning

in areas where you know you will be quilting.) Remove the tape, gently roll the pinned, layered half of the sandwich to the center, and repeat the process from the other end until the entire sandwich is pinned.

3. Unroll the sandwich, move any pins that might interfere with your quilting, and then close all the pins.

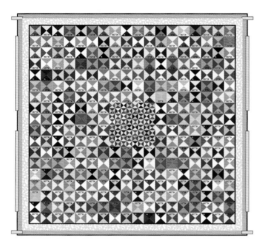

POINTS ON PINNING

If you feel a safety pin catch on your quilt top or backing, or have difficulty inserting it smoothly into position, throw the pin away. A blunted or roughened tip can break threads in the fabric and cause holes to appear. Most quilt shops and websites sell volume packs of small, rustproof safety pins that are perfect for pin basting. Buy more than you think you need so you won't run out halfway through the job.

Quilting

If you have quilted before, you know what to do when the instructions tell you to "quilt as desired." If you are new to quilting, invest in a well-illustrated book designed for a beginner, have a friend or relative show you how, or search for a good basic quilting site on the internet. For another wonderfully social alternative, enroll in a quilting class at a local shop or search out a quilt guild or church group that you can join.

Preparing the Binding

Many quilters underestimate the impact that the binding has on a quilt. Much like a picture frame, the binding makes an important design statement that can either enhance or undermine all your months of effort.

We both like a double-fold, mitered binding that finishes about ⅜" wide. It's a little wider than the standard ¼", but it works for us. We also take the time to carefully choose the fabric for the binding and audition *many* different choices. Color, pattern, compatibility, contrast, energy, and personality are all taken into consideration. Sometimes we end up using the same fabric for the binding that we used for the border, but by viewing lots of options, we can feel comfortable knowing we have made an informed choice.

1. Using your rotary cutter and your longest rotary ruler, carefully straighten the edges of your quilt, trimming the excess batting and backing even with the edges of the quilt top. Use a large square ruler to ensure that the corners of the quilt are square and trim them as necessary.

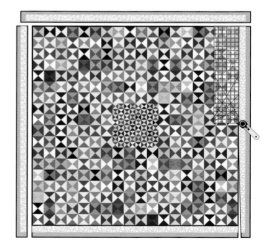

2. The instructions for each project tell you how many 2¾"-wide strips to cut for the binding (basically, the total perimeter of the quilt plus a minimum of 10" for mitered corners and seams). With right sides together, join the strips with diagonal

seams as shown. Trim the seam allowances to ¼" and press open.

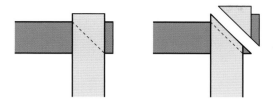

3. Fold the binding in half lengthwise, wrong sides together, and press. Unfold one end of the binding, make a diagonal fold toward the wrong side as shown, and press. Trim the excess fabric, leaving a ¼" seam allowance.

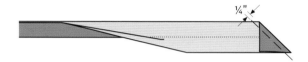

NOTIONS FOR BINDING

Consider purchasing a supply of quality sewing pins or binding clips before you get started on your binding. We like sewing pins with glass beads or plastic flowers on the ends; they're simply easier to manipulate. Binding clips are a quilter's best friend. Buy lots, since you'll use them! Of course, be prepared to toss away any pin or clip when it becomes blunt, worn, or snaggy.

Warning: Young girls love to use binding clips as hair clips, so if you have young girls at your house, you know where to look when you find your supply dwindling!

Attaching the Binding

We like to take our time sewing on bindings as they have great impact on the appearance of a finished quilt. Attention to precise measurements and extra pinning results in cleanly mitered and crisp, square corners. Use a walking foot on your machine if you have one; it helps prevent the top layers of fabric from shifting as you stitch. Here's what we do to attain the best results.

1. Leaving several inches free, and with right sides together and raw edges aligned, start pinning the binding to the quilt top 12" before a corner. Finish with a pin ¼" from the corner. Begin sewing the binding to the quilt with a generous ¼" seam, removing the pins just before the needle touches them. Stop with a backstitch at the final pin and cut the thread.

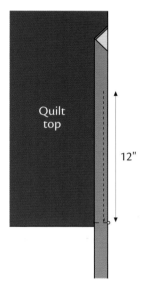

2. Turn the quilt so the bound edge is at the top. Fold the binding up so that the raw edge is aligned with the new side of the quilt and so that the fold makes a 45° angle as shown.

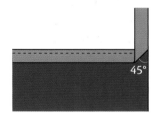

3. Maintaining the 45° angle, fold the binding back down on itself so the new fold is even with the top edge of the quilt and the raw edges of the binding are even with the side raw edge of the quilt as shown; pin.

Fold.

4. Verify the measurement of the side of the quilt and pin-mark the same measurement on the binding. Pin the binding to quilt, matching the center and end points and making any adjustments toward the center, rather than near the corners. Place a pin ¼" from the corner to mark your next stopping point. Beginning at the fold you made in step 3, resume sewing the binding to the quilt, stopping ¼" from the corner at the pin. Backstitch, turn the quilt, fold the binding, and continue in the same manner until you have turned the final corner.

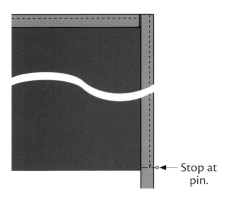

Stop at pin.

5. Stop sewing a few inches from the start of the binding and backstitch to anchor the seam. Leave the needle in the down position.

6. Raise the presser foot and pin the bottom layer of the starting end of the binding to the quilt as shown. Tuck the tail end of the binding into the opening to see how much excess you can trim to leave at least 1" of binding tail to tuck for a secure anchor. Trim the binding tail.

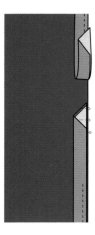

7. Carefully place the trimmed binding tail into the opening so there is a smooth and tidy overlap. Pin and stitch the last few inches of binding in place. Backstitch to anchor the threads.

8. Fold the binding over the edge to the back of the quilt and secure with binding clips or pins. Make sure the fold of the binding covers the stitching line. Slip-stitch the binding in place with a neutral or matching thread. We like to use quilt thread since it is less prone to tangling.

Quilt back

Adding a Label

Add a label to the back of your quilt that includes your name, address, date, and the title of the quilt (if it has one). If the quilt is a gift, you can add the name of the recipient too.

Biz Storms
100 Quilter's Lane
Toronto, Canada
"Guest Room Quilt"
Pieced by Biz Storms
Quilted by Emma Hostetler
November, 2007

BIBLIOGRAPHY

Horton, Laurel. "Blue Ridge Quiltmaking in the Late Twentieth Century." July 1999. 02 December 2007. http://memory.loc.gov/ammem/qlthtml/qltbr.html

Horton, Laurel. "Blue Ridge Quilters: Mamie Bryan." July 1999. 02 December 2007. http://memory.loc.gov/ammem/qlthtml/qltmb.html

Horton, Laurel. "Blue Ridge Quilters: Maggie Shockley." July 1999. 02 December 2007. http://memory.loc.gov/ammem/qlthtml/qltms.html

Kiracofe, Roderick. *The American Quilt: A History of Cloth and Comfort*. New York: Clarkson Potter, 1993.

Marston, Gwen. *Gwen Marston's Needlework Designs*. Paducah, Kentucky: American Quilter's Society, 2006.

Marston, Gwen. *Liberated Quiltmaking*. Paducah, Kentucky: Collector Books, 1997.

Marston, Gwen and Joe Cunningham. *Quilting With Style: Principles for Great Pattern Design*. Paducah, Kentucky: American Quilter's Society, 1993.

Moonen, An. *Quilts een Nederlandse traditie/Quilts in the Dutch tradition*. Arnhem, Nederlands: Nederlands Openluchtmuseum, 1992.

Moran, Freddy and Gwen Marston. *Collaborative Quilting*. New York: Sterling Publishing Company, 2006.

Nelson, Cyril I. and Carter Houck. *Treasury of American Quilts*. New York: Greenwich House, 1984.

Oliver, Celia Y. *Enduring Grace: Quilts from the Shelburne Museum Collection*. Lafayette, California: C&T Publishing, 1997.

Rae, Janet. *The Quilts of the British Isles*. New York: E. P. Dutton, 1987.

Reich, Sue. "Multitudinous Scrap Quilts," *Fons and Porter's Love of Quilting*, January–February 2007: pp. 54–56.

Reich, Sue. *Quilting News of Yesteryear: 1,000 Pieces and Counting*. Atglen, Pennsylvania: Schiffer Publishing Ltd., 2007.

The Quilter's Guild. *Quilt Treasures: The Quilter's Guild Heritage Search*. London, England: Deirdre Mcdonald Books, 1995.

Wettre, Asa. *Old Swedish Quilts*. Loveland, Colorado: Interweave Press, 1995.

Woodward. Thos. K. and Blanche Greenstein. *Crib Quilts and Other Small Wonders*. New York: E. P. Dutton, 1981.

RESOURCES

In this day and age, we have a wonderful resource in the internet. It is a great place to source products and find quilting information. Many prominent quiltmakers and most suppliers have Web sites chock-a-block with information, ideas, and inspiration. Have fun exploring. Here are a few that have been integral to us for this book:

Amish Handquilting Services
http://www.amishhandquilting.com

Amish Quilting Service
http://amishquilting.net/

National Gallery of Australia
http://nga.gov.au/RajahQuilt/

Paper Pieces
1-800-337-1537
www.paperpieces.com

The Quilt Index
http://www.quiltindex.org

The Shelburne Museum
http://www.shelburnemuseum.org

The Susan McCord Quilts
http://www.si.umich.edu/chico/quilts/

ACKNOWLEDGMENTS

Our thanks go to:

Darra Williamson, wordsmith extraordinaire, for her support and commitment to this project from its infancy.

The editors and staff at Martingale—it's been such fun, we would do it again!

Amberlea Williams, who not only earned a pair of wings but showed herself as a fine needlewoman, too!

Kory Rogers and Julie Sopher of the Shelburne Museum. (Kory, we are quite sure the tires did not touch the ground all the way home after our visit with you at the Shelburne.)

Fumie Ono for graciously answering the request of a fledging quilt author and lending photographs of her quilt for this book.

Margaret Mitchell—the quilt looks fabulous and we thank you for all your gorgeous work over the years.

Sandra Reed for being there when Murphy's Law happened, and for spoiling us with her wonderful, award-winning featherwork.

Nancy Ray for her support, her humor, and for laughing with us at BFOOs (Blinding Flashes of the Obvious).

Our quilting friends Catherine, Kathy, Judy, Jennifer, Myrna, Helgard, and all of the women of Beaver Island Quilting Retreat.

Sonya Gotziaman for her invaluable support.

Paul Papoutsakis and Karen Hewlett for keeping us moving and happy.

We couldn't have written this book and made these quilts without the support of our families. Thank you Alan, Turner, Peter, Jamie, Iain, Emma, Mom and Dad, and the rest of the clans.

And to Gwen, for always providing amazing ideas and inspiration at her Beaver Island Quilt Retreats and for blessing us with her quilt for this book.

ABOUT THE AUTHORS

Mary Elizabeth Kinch

Mary Elizabeth started quilting in 1975 while work-ing as an historical interpreter at Black Creek Pioneer Village. Passionate about creativity since she was very young and always fascinated with fabric and color, she obtained one of her degrees in fashion design. A life-long exposure to the arts and antiques has contributed to her love of design and her fondness for the antique quilts she studies and collects.

Mary Elizabeth presently designs interior environ-ments, and she encourages others to tap their own creative abilities. Mary Elizabeth lives in Toronto with her most cherished treasures, her three children. The family dog loves to visit with Biz's three dogs!

Biz Storms

After 15 years in advertising, Biz redirected her life to marriage and children. A crib quilt for her daughter led to the world of quilting and eventually to writing quilt books.

Beyond her enthusiasm for quilting and collecting antique quilts, Biz and her husband share a love for dressage (a form of exhibition riding) and for Shaker-hill, their country farm. Biz is equally passionate about heirloom apples, having created an orchard with over 500 varieties of apples, plus medlars (a small, brown, applelike fruit), quince, and perry pears. Bee keeping, making hard cider, and breeding red flesh apples also keep her busy.

Biz and her family live in Toronto with their three dogs. The horses stay at the farm!

New and Best-Selling Titles from

America's Best-Loved
Quilt Books®

America's Best-Loved Craft & Hobby Books®
America's Best-Loved Knitting Books®

APPLIQUÉ
Applique Quilt Revival
Beautiful Blooms
Cutting-Garden Quilts
Dream Landscapes—*NEW!*
More Fabulous Flowers
Sunbonnet Sue and Scottie Too

BABIES AND CHILDREN
Baby's First Quilts—*NEW!*
Baby Wraps
Even More Quilts for Baby
Let's Pretend—*NEW!*
The Little Box of Baby Quilts
Snuggle-and-Learn Quilts for Kids
Sweet and Simple Baby Quilts

BEGINNER
Color for the Terrified Quilter
Happy Endings, Revised Edition
Machine Appliqué for the Terrified Quilter
Your First Quilt Book (or it should be!)

GENERAL QUILTMAKING
Adventures in Circles
American Jane's Quilts for All Seasons—*NEW!*
Bits and Pieces
Charmed
Cool Girls Quilt
Country-Fresh Quilts—*NEW!*
Creating Your Perfect Quilting Space
Follow-the-Line Quilting Designs Volume Three
Gathered from the Garden
The New Handmade—*NEW!*
Points of View
Positively Postcards
Prairie Children and Their Quilts
Quilt Revival
A Quilter's Diary
Quilter's Happy Hour
Quilting for Joy—*NEW!*
Sensational Sashiko
Simple Seasons
Skinny Quilts and Table Runners

Twice Quilted
Young at Heart Quilts

HOLIDAY AND SEASONAL
Christmas Quilts from Hopscotch
Christmas with Artful Offerings
Comfort and Joy
Holiday Wrappings

HOOKED RUGS, NEEDLE FELTING, AND PUNCHNEEDLE
The Americana Collection
Miniature Punchneedle Embroidery
Needle-Felting Magic
Needle Felting with Cotton and Wool
Punchneedle Fun

PAPER PIECING
Easy Reversible Vests, Revised Edition—*NEW!*
Paper-Pieced Mini Quilts
Show Me How to Paper Piece
Showstopping Quilts to Foundation Piece
A Year of Paper Piecing

PIECING
501 Rotary-Cut Quilt Blocks—*NEW!*
Better by the Dozen
Favorite Traditional Quilts Made Easy—*NEW!*
Loose Change—*NEW!*
Maple Leaf Quilts
Mosaic Picture Quilts
New Cuts for New Quilts
Nine by Nine
On-Point Quilts
Quiltastic Curves
Ribbon Star Quilts
Rolling Along
Sew One and You're Done

QUICK QUILTS
40 Fabulous Quick-Cut Quilts
Instant Bargello
Quilts on the Double
Sew Fun, Sew Colorful Quilts

SCRAP QUILTS
Nickel Quilts
Save the Scraps
Simple Strategies for Scrap Quilts
Spotlight on Scraps

CRAFTS
Art from the Heart
The Beader's Handbook
Card Design
Crochet for Beaders
Dolly Mama Beads
Embellished Memories—*NEW!*
Friendship Bracelets All Grown Up
Making Beautiful Jewelry—*NEW!*
Paper It!—*NEW!*
Sculpted Threads
Sew Sentimental
Trading Card Treasures—*NEW!*

KNITTING & CROCHET
365 Crochet Stitches a Year
365 Knitting Stitches a Year
A to Z of Knitting
All about Knitting—*NEW!*
Amigurumi World
Beyond Wool—*NEW!*
Cable Confidence
Casual, Elegant Knits
Chic Knits
Crocheted Pursenalities
Gigi Knits…and Purls
Kitty Knits
Knitted Finger Puppets—*NEW!*
The Knitter's Book of Finishing Techniques
Knitting Circles around Socks
Knitting with Gigi
More Sensational Knitted Socks
Pursenalities
Skein for Skein
Toe-Up Techniques for Hand Knit Socks, Revised Edition—*NEW!*
Together or Separate—*NEW!*

Our books are available at bookstores and your favorite craft, fabric, and yarn retailers. If you don't see the title you're looking for, visit us at **www.martingale-pub.com** or contact us at:

1-800-426-3126

International: 1-425-483-3313
Fax: 1-425-486-7596 • Email: info@martingale-pub.com